I0224450

THE
TWELVE-POUND LOOK
AND OTHER PLAYS

THE
TWELVE-POUND
LOOK

AND OTHER PLAYS

J. M. BARRIE

Fredonia Books
Amsterdam, The Netherlands

The Twelve-Pound Look

by
J. M. Barrie

ISBN: 1-4101-0240-8

Copyright © 2003 by Fredonia Books

Reprinted from the 1921 edition

Fredonia Books
Amsterdam, The Netherlands
http://www.fredoniabooks.com

All rights reserved, including the right to reproduce
this book, or portions thereof, in any form.

In order to make original editions of historical works
available to scholars at an economical price, this
facsimile of the original edition of 1921 is
reproduced from the best available copy and has
been digitally enhanced to improve legibility, but the
text remains unaltered to retain historical
authenticity.

CONTENTS

THE TWELVE-POUND LOOK

THE TWELVE-POUND LOOK

*If quite convenient (as they say about cheques) you
are to conceive that the scene is laid in your own
house, and that Harry Sims is you. Perhaps the
ornamentation of the house is a trifle ostentatious,
but if you cavil at that we are willing to re-decorate :
you don't get out of being Harry Sims on a mere
matter of plush and dados. It pleases us to make
him a city man, but (rather than lose you) he can be
turned with a scrape of the pen into a K.C., fashionable doctor, Secretary of State, or what you will. We
conceive him of a pleasant rotundity with a thick red
neck, but we shall waive that point if you know him
to be thin.*

*It is that day in your career when everything went
wrong just when everything seemed to be superlatively
right.*

*In Harry's case it was a woman who did the
mischief. She came to him in his great hour and told
him she did not admire him. Of course he turned
her out of the house and was soon himself again, but*

*it spoilt the morning for him. This is the subject
of the play, and quite enough too.*

*Harry is to receive the honour of knighthood in
a few days, and we discover him in the sumptuous
' snuggery ' of his home in Kensington (or is it
Westminster?), rehearsing the ceremony with his
wife. They have been at it all the morning, a pleasing
occupation. Mrs. Sims (as we may call her for the
last time, as it were, and strictly as a good-natured
joke) is wearing her presentation gown, and personates
the august one who is about to dub her Harry knight.
She is seated regally. Her jewelled shoulders pro-
claim aloud her husband's generosity. She must
be an extraordinarily proud and happy woman, yet
she has a drawn face and shrinking ways as if there
were some one near her of whom she is afraid. She
claps her hands, as the signal to Harry. He enters
bowing, and with a graceful swerve of the leg. He is
only partly in costume, the sword and the real stockings
not having arrived yet. With a gliding motion that
is only delayed while one leg makes up on the other,
he reaches his wife, and, going on one knee, raises
her hand superbly to his lips. She taps him on the
shoulder with a paper-knife and says huskily, ' Rise,
Sir Harry.' He rises, bows, and glides about the
room, going on his knees to various articles of furniture,*

and rising from each a knight. It is a radiant domestic scene, and Harry is as dignified as if he knew that royalty was rehearsing it at the other end.

SIR HARRY (*complacently*). Did that seem all right, eh ?

LADY SIMS (*much relieved*). I think perfect.

SIR HARRY. But was it dignified ?

LADY SIMS. Oh, very. And it will be still more so when you have the sword.

SIR HARRY. The sword will lend it an air. There are really the five moments—(*suiting the action to the word*)—the glide—the dip—the kiss—the tap—and you back out a knight. It 's short, but it 's a very beautiful ceremony. (*Kindly*) Anything you can suggest ?

LADY SIMS. No—oh no. (*Nervously, seeing him pause to kiss the tassel of a cushion*) You don't think you have practised till you know what to do almost too well ?

> (*He has been in a blissful temper, but such niggling criticism would try any man.*)

SIR HARRY. I do not. Don't talk nonsense. Wait till your opinion is asked for.

LADY SIMS (*abashed*). I 'm sorry, Harry. (*A*

perfect butler appears and presents a card.) ' The Flora Type-Writing Agency.'

SIR HARRY.   Ah, yes.   I telephoned them to send some one.   A woman, I suppose, Tombes ?

TOMBES.   Yes, Sir Harry.

SIR HARRY.   Show her in here.   (*He has very lately become a stickler for etiquette.*)   And, Tombes, strictly speaking, you know, I am not Sir Harry till Thursday.

TOMBES.   Beg pardon, sir, but it is such a satisfaction to us.

SIR HARRY (*good-naturedly*).   Ah, they like it downstairs, do they ?

TOMBES (*unbending*).   Especially the females, Sir Harry.

SIR HARRY.   Exactly.   You can show her in, Tombes.   (*The butler departs on his mighty task.*)   You can tell the woman what she is wanted for, Emmy, while I change.   (*He is too modest to boast about himself, and prefers to keep a wife in the house for that purpose.*)   You can tell her the sort of things about me that will come better from you.   (*Smiling happily*)   You heard what Tombes said, ' Especially the females.' And he is right. Success! The women like it even better than the men. And rightly. For they share. *You* share, *Lady* Sims. Not a woman will see that gown without being sick with envy of it. I know them. Have all our lady friends in to see it. It will make them ill for a week.

> (*These sentiments carry him off light-heartedly, and presently the disturbing element is shown in. She is a mere typist, dressed in uncommonly good taste, but at contemptibly small expense, and she is carrying her typewriter in a friendly way rather than as a badge of slavery, as of course it is. Her eye is clear; and in odd contrast to* LADY SIMS, *she is self-reliant and serene.*)

KATE (*respectfully, but she should have waited to be spoken to*). Good morning, madam.

LADY SIMS (*in her nervous way, and scarcely noticing that the typist is a little too ready with her tongue*). Good morning. (*As a first impression she rather likes the woman, and the woman, though it is scarcely worth mentioning, rather*

likes her. LADY SIMS *has a maid for buttoning
and unbuttoning her, and probably another for
waiting on the maid, and she gazes with a little
envy perhaps at a woman who does things for
herself.*) Is that the type-writing machine ?

KATE (*who is getting it ready for use*). Yes
(*not ' Yes, madam,' as it ought to be*). I suppose
if I am to work here I may take this off. I get
on better without it. (*She is referring to her hat.*)

LADY SIMS. Certainly. (*But the hat is already
off.*) I ought to apologise for my gown. I am
to be presented this week, and I was trying it on.
(*Her tone is not really apologetic. She is rather
clinging to the glory of her gown, wistfully, as if
not absolutely certain, you know, that it is a glory.*)

KATE. It is beautiful, if I may presume to say
so. (*She frankly admires it. She probably has
a best, and a second best of her own : that sort of
thing.*)

LADY SIMS (*with a flush of pride in the gown*).
Yes, it is very beautiful. (*The beauty of it gives
her courage.*) Sit down, please.

KATE (*the sort of woman who would have sat
down in any case*). I suppose it is some copying

you want done ? I got no particulars. I was told to come to this address, but that was all.

LADY SIMS (*almost with the humility of a servant*). Oh, it is not work for me, it is for my husband, and what he needs is not exactly copying. (*Swelling, for she is proud of* HARRY.) He wants a number of letters answered—hundreds of them—letters and telegrams of congratulation.

KATE (*as if it were all in the day's work*). Yes ?

LADY SIMS (*remembering that* HARRY *expects every wife to do her duty*). My husband is a remarkable man. He is about to be knighted. (*Pause, but* KATE *does not fall to the floor.*) He is to be knighted for his services to—(*on reflection*)—for his services. (*She is conscious that she is not doing* HARRY *justice.*) He can explain it so much better than I can.

KATE (*in her business-like way*). And I am to answer the congratulations ?

LADY SIMS (*afraid that it will be a hard task*). Yes.

KATE (*blithely*). It is work I have had some experience of. (*She proceeds to type.*)

LADY SIMS. But you can't begin till you know what he wants to say.

KATE. Only a specimen letter. Won't it be the usual thing ?

LADY SIMS (*to whom this is a new idea*). Is there a usual thing ?

KATE. Oh, yes.

> (*She continues to type, and* LADY SIMS, *half-mesmerised, gazes at her nimble fingers. The useless woman watches the useful one, and she sighs, she could not tell why.*)

LADY SIMS. How quickly you do it. It must be delightful to be able to do something, and to do it well.

KATE (*thankfully*). Yes, it is delightful.

LADY SIMS (*again remembering the source of all her greatness*). But, excuse me, I don't think that will be any use. My husband wants me to explain to you that his is an exceptional case. He did not try to get this honour in any way. It was a complete surprise to him——

KATE (*who is a practical Kate and no dealer in sarcasm*). That is what I have written.

LADY SIMS (*in whom sarcasm would meet a dead wall*). But how could you know?

KATE. I only guessed.

LADY SIMS. Is that the usual thing?

KATE. Oh, yes.

LADY SIMS. They don't try to get it?

KATE. I don't know. That is what we are told to say in the letters.

> (*To her at present the only important thing about the letters is that they are ten shillings the hundred.*)

LADY SIMS (*returning to surer ground*). I should explain that my husband is not a man who cares for honours. So long as he does his duty——

KATE. Yes, I have been putting that in.

LADY SIMS. Have you? But he particularly wants it to be known that he would have declined a title were it not——

KATE. I have got it here.

LADY SIMS. What have you got?

KATE (*reading*). 'Indeed I would have asked to be allowed to decline had it not been that I want to please my wife.'

LADY SIMS (*heavily*).   But how could you know it was that ?

KATE.   Is it ?

LADY SIMS (*who after all is the one with the right to ask questions*).   Do they all accept it for that reason ?

KATE.   That is what we are told to say in the letters.

LADY SIMS (*thoughtlessly*).   It is quite as if you knew my husband.

KATE.   I assure you, I don't even know his name.

LADY SIMS (*suddenly showing that she knows him*).   Oh, he wouldn't like that.

> (*And it is here that* HARRY *re-enters in his city garments, looking so gay, feeling so jolly that we bleed for him. However, the annoying* KATHERINE *is to get a shock also.*)

LADY SIMS.   This is the lady, Harry.

SIR HARRY (*shooting his cuffs*).   Yes, yes. Good morning, my dear.

> (*Then they see each other, and their mouths open, but not for words. After the first surprise* KATE *seems to find some humour*

in the situation, but HARRY *lowers like a thundercloud.*)

LADY SIMS (*who has seen nothing*).   I have been trying to explain to her——

SIR HARRY. Eh—what ? (*He controls himself.*) Leave it to me, Emmy ; I'll attend to her.

(LADY SIMS *goes, with a dread fear that somehow she has vexed her lord, and then* HARRY *attends to the intruder.*)

SIR HARRY (*with concentrated scorn*).   You !

KATE (*as if agreeing with him*). Yes, it's funny.

SIR HARRY.   The shamelessness of your daring to come here.

KATE.   Believe me, it is not less a surprise to me than it is to you. I was sent here in the ordinary way of business. I was given only the number of the house. I was not told the name.

SIR HARRY (*withering her*).   The ordinary way of business ! This is what you have fallen to—a typist !

KATE (*unwithered*).   Think of it.

SIR HARRY.   After going through worse straits, I 'll be bound.

KATE (*with some grim memories*).   Much worse straits.

SIR HARRY (*alas, laughing coarsely*).   My congratulations.

KATE.   Thank you, Harry.

SIR HARRY (*who is annoyed, as any man would be, not to find her abject*).   Eh ?   What was that you called me, madam ?

KATE.   Isn't it Harry ?   On my soul, I almost forget.

SIR HARRY.   It isn't Harry to you.   My name is Sims, if you please.

KATE.   Yes, I had not forgotten that.   It was my name, too, you see.

SIR HARRY (*in his best manner*).   It was your name till you forfeited the right to bear it.

KATE.   Exactly.

SIR HARRY (*gloating*).   I was furious to find you here, but on second thoughts it pleases me. (*From the depths of his moral nature*) There is a grim justice in this.

KATE (*sympathetically*).   Tell me ?

SIR HARRY. Do you know what you were brought here to do?

KATE. I have just been learning. You have been made a knight, and I was summoned to answer the messages of congratulation.

SIR HARRY. That's it, that's it. You come on this day as my servant!

KATE. I, who might have been Lady Sims.

SIR HARRY. And you are her typist instead. And she has four men-servants. Oh, I am glad you saw her in her presentation gown.

KATE. I wonder if she would let me do her washing, Sir Harry?

(*Her want of taste disgusts him.*)

SIR HARRY (*with dignity*). You can go. The mere thought that only a few flights of stairs separates such as you from my innocent children——

> (*He will never know why a new light has come into her face.*)

KATE (*slowly*). You have children?

SIR HARRY (*inflated*). Two.

> (*He wonders why she is so long in answering.*)

KATE (*resorting to impertinence*),   Such a nice number.

SIR HARRY (*with an extra turn of the screw*). Both boys.

KATE.   Successful in everything. Are they like you, Sir Harry ?

SIR HARRY (*expanding*). They are very like me.

KATE.   That 's nice.

(*Even on such a subject as this she can be ribald.*)

SIR HARRY.   Will you please to go.

KATE.   Heigho ! What shall I say to my employer ?

SIR HARRY.   That is no affair of mine.

KATE. What will you say to Lady Sims ?

SIR HARRY. I flatter myself that whatever I say, Lady Sims will accept without comment.

(*She smiles, heaven knows why, unless her next remark explains it.*)

KATE.   Still the same Harry.

SIR HARRY.   What do you mean ?

KATE.   Only that you have the old confidence in your profound knowledge of the sex.

SIR HARRY (*beginning to think as little of her*

intellect as of her morals). I suppose I know my wife.

KATE (*hopelessly dense*). I suppose so. I was only remembering that you used to think you knew her in the days when I was the lady. (*He is merely wasting his time on her, and he indicates the door. She is not sufficiently the lady to retire worsted.*) Well, good-bye, Sir Harry. Won't you ring, and the four men-servants will show me out ?

(*But he hesitates.*)

SIR HARRY (*in spite of himself*). As you are here, there is something I want to get out of you. (*Wishing he could ask it less eagerly*) Tell me, who was the man ?

(*The strange woman—it is evident now that she has always been strange to him—smiles tolerantly.*)

KATE. You never found out ?

SIR HARRY. I could never be sure.

KATE (*reflectively*). I thought that would worry you.

SIR HARRY (*sneering*). It's plain that he soon left you.

B

KATE.   Very soon.

SIR HARRY.   As I could have told you.   (*But still she surveys him with the smile of Mona Lisa. The badgered man has to entreat.*)   Who was he?   It was fourteen years ago, and cannot matter to any of us now.   Kate, tell me who he was?

> (*It is his first youthful moment, and perhaps because of that she does not wish to hurt him.*)

KATE (*shaking a motherly head*).   Better not ask.

SIR HARRY.   I do ask.   Tell me.

KATE.   It is kinder not to tell you.

SIR HARRY (*violently*).   Then, by James, it was one of my own pals.   Was it Bernard Roche?   (*She shakes her head.*)   It may have been some one who comes to my house still.

KATE.   I think not.   (*Reflecting*)   Fourteen years!   You found my letter that night when you went home?

SIR HARRY (*impatient*).   Yes.

KATE.   I propped it against the decanters. I thought you would be sure to see it there.   It was a room not unlike this, and the furniture was arranged in the same attractive way. How it all comes back to me. Don't you see me, Harry, in hat and cloak, putting the letter there, taking a last look round, and then stealing out into the night to meet——

SIR HARRY. Whom?

KATE. Him. Hours pass, no sound in the room but the tick-tack of the clock, and then about midnight you return alone. You take——

SIR HARRY (*gruffly*). I wasn't alone.

KATE (*the picture spoilt*). No? oh. (*Plaintively*) Here have I all these years been conceiving it wrongly. (*She studies his face.*) I believe something interesting happened?

SIR HARRY (*growling*). Something confoundedly annoying.

KATE (*coaxing*). Do tell me.

SIR HARRY. We won't go into that. Who was the man? Surely a husband has a right to know with whom his wife bolted.

KATE (*who is detestably ready with her tongue*). Surely the wife has a right to know how he took it. (*The woman's love of bargaining comes to her aid.*) A fair exchange. You tell me what happened, and I will tell you who he was.

SIR HARRY. You will ? Very well. (*It is the first point on which they have agreed, and, forgetting himself, he takes a place beside her on the fire-seat. He is thinking only of what he is to tell her, but she, woman-like, is conscious of their proximity.*)

KATE (*tastelessly*). Quite like old times. (*He moves away from her indignantly.*) Go on, Harry.

SIR HARRY (*who has a manful shrinking from saying anything that is to his disadvantage*). Well, as you know, I was dining at the club that night.

KATE. Yes.

SIR HARRY. Jack Lamb drove me home. Mabbett Green was with us, and I asked them to come in for a few minutes.

KATE. Jack Lamb, Mabbett Green ? I think I remember them. Jack was in Parliament.

SIR HARRY. No, that was Mabbett. They came into the house with me and—(*with sudden horror*)—was it him ?

KATE (*bewildered*). Who ?

SIR HARRY. Mabbett ?

KATE. What ?

SIR HARRY. The man ?

KATE. What man ? (*Understanding*) Oh no.
I thought you said he came into the house with
you.

SIR HARRY. It might have been a blind.

KATE. Well, it wasn't. Go on.

SIR HARRY. They came in to finish a talk we
had been having at the club.

KATE. An interesting talk, evidently.

SIR HARRY. The papers had been full that
evening of the elopement of some countess
woman with a fiddler. What was her name ?

KATE. Does it matter ?

SIR HARRY. No. (*Thus ends the countess.*)
We had been discussing the thing and—(*he pulls
a wry face*)—and I had been rather warm——

KATE (*with horrid relish*). I begin to see.
You had been saying it served the husband right,
that the man who could not look after his wife
deserved to lose her. It was one of your favourite subjects. Oh, Harry, say it was that !

SIR HARRY (*sourly*).   It may have been something like that.

KATE.   And all the time the letter was there, waiting ; and none of you knew except the clock. Harry, it is sweet of you to tell me. (*His face is not sweet. The illiterate woman has used the wrong adjective.*)   I forget what I said precisely in the letter.

SIR HARRY (*pulverising her*).   So do I. But I have it still.

KATE (*not pulverised*).   Do let me see it again. (*She has observed his eye wandering to the desk.*)

SIR HARRY.   You are welcome to it as a gift. (*The fateful letter, a poor little dead thing, is brought to light from a locked drawer.*)

KATE (*taking it*).   Yes, this is it. Harry, how you did crumple it ! (*She reads, not without curiosity.*)   ' Dear husband—I call you that for the last time—I am off. I am what you call making a bolt of it. I won't try to excuse myself nor to explain, for you would not accept the excuses nor understand the explanation. It will be a little shock to you, but only to your pride; what will astound you is that any woman could be such a fool as to leave such a man as you. I am taking nothing with me that belongs to you. May you be very happy.—Your ungrateful KATE. *P.S.*—You need not try to find out who he is. You will try, but you won't succeed.' (*She folds the nasty little thing up.*) I may really have it for my very own ?

SIR HARRY. You really may.

KATE (*impudently*). If you would care for a typed copy—— ?

SIR HARRY (*in a voice with which he used to frighten his grandmother*). None of your sauce. (*Wincing*) I had to let them see it in the end.

KATE. I can picture Jack Lamb eating it.

SIR HARRY. A penniless parson's daughter.

KATE. That is all I was.

SIR HARRY. We searched for the two of you high and low.

KATE. Private detectives ?

SIR HARRY. They couldn't get on the track of you.

KATE (*smiling*). No ?

SIR HARRY. But at last the courts let me

serve the papers by advertisement on a man unknown, and I got my freedom.

KATE. So I saw. It was the last I heard of you.

SIR HARRY (*each word a blow for her*). And I married again just as soon as ever I could.

KATE. They say that is always a compliment to the first wife.

SIR HARRY (*violently*). I showed them.

KATE. You soon let them see that if one woman was a fool, you still had the pick of the basket to choose from.

SIR HARRY. By James, I did.

KATE (*bringing him to earth again*). But still, you wondered who he was.

SIR HARRY. I suspected everybody—even my pals. I felt like jumping at their throats and crying, ' It 's you ! '

KATE. You had been so admirable to me, an instinct told you that I was sure to choose another of the same.

SIR HARRY. I thought, it can't be money, so it must be looks. Some dolly face. (*He stares at her in perplexity.*) He must have had something wonderful about him to make you willing to give up all that you had with me.

KATE (*as if he was the stupid one*). Poor Harry.

SIR HARRY. And it couldn't have been going on for long, for I would have noticed the change in you.

KATE. Would you ?

SIR HARRY. I knew you so well.

KATE. You amazing man.

SIR HARRY. So who was he ? Out with it.

KATE. You are determined to know ?

SIR HARRY. Your promise. You gave your word.

KATE. If I must—— (*She is the villain of the piece, but it must be conceded that in this matter she is reluctant to pain him.*) I am sorry I promised. (*Looking at him steadily.*) There was no one, Harry ; no one at all.

SIR HARRY (*rising*). If you think you can play with me——

KATE. I told you that you wouldn't like it.

SIR HARRY (*rasping*). It is unbelievable.

KATE. I suppose it is ; but it is true.

SIR HARRY. Your letter itself gives you the lie.

KATE. That was intentional. I saw that if the truth were known you might have a difficulty in getting your freedom ; and as I was getting mine it seemed fair that you should have yours also. So I wrote my good-bye in words that would be taken to mean what you thought they meant, and I knew the law would back you in your opinion. For the law, like you, Harry, has a profound understanding of women.

SIR HARRY (*trying to straighten himself*). I don't believe you yet.

KATE (*looking not unkindly into the soul of this man*). Perhaps that is the best way to take it. It is less unflattering than the truth. But you were the only one. (*Summing up her life.*) You sufficed.

SIR HARRY. Then what mad impulse——

KATE. It was no impulse, Harry. I had thought it out for a year.

SIR HARRY. A year ? (*dazed*). One would think to hear you that I hadn't been a good husband to you.

KATE (*with a sad smile*). You were a good husband according to your lights.

SIR HARRY (*stoutly*). *I* think so.

KATE. And a moral man, and chatty, and quite the philanthropist.

SIR HARRY (*on sure ground*). All women envied you.

KATE. How you loved me to be envied.

SIR HARRY. I swaddled you in luxury.

KATE (*making her great revelation*). That was it.

SIR HARRY (*blankly*). What?

KATE (*who can be serene because it is all over*). How you beamed at me when I sat at the head of your fat dinners in my fat jewellery, surrounded by our fat friends.

SIR HARRY (*aggrieved*). They weren't so fat.

KATE (*a side issue*). All except those who were so thin. Have you ever noticed, Harry, that many jewels make women either incredibly fat or incredibly thin?

SIR HARRY (*shouting*). I have not. (*Is it worth while to argue with her any longer?*) We had all the most interesting society of the day.

It wasn't only business men. There were politicians, painters, writers——

KATE.   Only the glorious, dazzling successes. Oh, the fat talk while we ate too much—about who had made a hit and who was slipping back, and what the noo house cost and the noo motor and the gold soup-plates, and who was to be the noo knight.

SIR HARRY (*who it will be observed is unanswerable from first to last*).   Was anybody getting on better than me, and consequently you ?

KATE.   Consequently me !   Oh, Harry, you and your sublime religion.

SIR HARRY (*honest heart*).   My religion ?   I never was one to talk about religion, but——

KATE.   Pooh, Harry, you don't even know what your religion was and is and will be till the day of your expensive funeral. (*And here is the lesson that life has taught her.*) One's religion is whatever he is most interested in, and yours is Success.

SIR HARRY (*quoting from his morning paper*). Ambition—it is the last infirmity of noble minds.

KATE.   Noble minds !

SIR HARRY (*at last grasping what she is talking about*). You are not saying that you left me because of my success ?

KATE. Yes, that was it. (*And now she stands revealed to him.*) I couldn't endure it. If a failure had come now and then—but your success was suffocating me. (*She is rigid with emotion.*) The passionate craving I had to be done with it, to find myself among people who had not got on.

SIR HARRY (*with proper spirit*). There are plenty of them.

KATE. There were none in our set. When they began to go down-hill they rolled out of our sight.

SIR HARRY (*clinching it*). I tell you I am worth a quarter of a million.

KATE (*unabashed*). That is what you are worth to yourself. I 'll tell you what you are worth to me : exactly twelve pounds. For I made up my mind that I could launch myself on the world alone if I first proved my mettle by earning twelve pounds ; and as soon as I had earned it I left you.

SIR HARRY (*in the scales*). Twelve pounds !

KATE. That is your value to a woman. If she can't make it she has to stick to you.

SIR HARRY (*remembering perhaps a rectory garden*). You valued me at more than that when you married me.

KATE (*seeing it also*). Ah, I didn't know you then. If only you had been a man, Harry.

SIR HARRY. A man ? What do you mean by a man ?

KATE (*leaving the garden*). Haven't you heard of them ? They are something fine ; and every woman is loath to admit to herself that her husband is not one. When she marries, even though she has been a very trivial person, there is in her some vague stirring toward a worthy life, as well as a fear of her capacity for evil. She knows her chance lies in him. If there is something good in him, what is good in her finds it, and they join forces against the baser parts. So I didn't give you up willingly, Harry. I invented all sorts of theories to explain you. Your hardness—I said it was a fine want of mawkishness. Your coarseness—

I said it goes with strength. Your contempt for the weak—I called it virility. Your want of ideals was clear-sightedness. Your ignoble views of women—I tried to think them funny. Oh, I clung to you to save myself. But I had to let go ; you had only the one quality, Harry, success ; you had it so strong that it swallowed all the others.

SIR HARRY (*not to be diverted from the main issue*). How did you earn that twelve pounds ?

KATE. It took me nearly six months ; but I earned it fairly. (*She presses her hand on the typewriter as lovingly as many a woman has pressed a rose.*) I learned this. I hired it and taught myself. I got some work through a friend, and with my first twelve pounds I paid for my machine. Then I considered that I was free to go, and I went.

SIR HARRY. All this going on in my house while you were living in the lap of luxury ! (*She nods.*) By God, you were determined.

KATE (*briefly*). By God, I was.

SIR HARRY (*staring*). How you must have hated me.

KATE (*smiling at the childish word*). Not a bit—after I saw that there was a way out. From that hour you amused me, Harry; I was even sorry for you, for I saw that you couldn't help yourself. Success is just a fatal gift.

SIR HARRY. Oh, thank you.

KATE (*thinking, dear friends in front, of you and me perhaps*). Yes, and some of your most successful friends knew it. One or two of them used to look very sad at times, as if they thought they might have come to something if they hadn't got on.

SIR HARRY (*who has a horror of sacrilege*). The battered crew you live among now—what are they but folk who have tried to succeed and failed ?

KATE. That's it ; they try, but they fail.

SIR HARRY. And always will fail.

KATE. Always. Poor souls—I say of them. Poor soul—they say of me. It keeps us human. That is why I never tire of them.

SIR HARRY (*comprehensively*). Bah ! Kate, I tell you I 'll be worth half a million yet.

KATE. I 'm sure you will. You 're getting stout, Harry.

SIR HARRY. No, I 'm not.

KATE. What was the name of that fat old fellow who used to fall asleep at our dinner-parties ?

SIR HARRY. If you mean Sir William Crackley——

KATE. That was the man. Sir William was to me a perfect picture of the grand success. He had got on so well that he was very, very stout, and when he sat on a chair it was thus (*her hands meeting in front of her*)—as if he were holding his success together. That is what you are working for, Harry. You will have that and the half million about the same time.

SIR HARRY (*who has surely been very patient*). Will you please to leave my house.

KATE (*putting on her gloves, soiled things*). But don't let us part in anger. How do you think I am looking, Harry, compared to the dull, inert thing that used to roll round in your padded carriages ?

SIR HARRY (*in masterly fashion*). I forget

c

what you were like. I 'm very sure you never could have held a candle to the present Lady Sims.

KATE. That is a picture of her, is it not ?

SIR HARRY (*seizing his chance again*). In her wedding-gown. Painted by an R.A.

KATE (*wickedly*). A knight ?

SIR HARRY (*deceived*). Yes.

KATE (*who likes* LADY SIMS: *a piece of presumption on her part*). It is a very pretty face.

SIR HARRY (*with the pride of possession*). Acknowledged to be a beauty everywhere.

KATE. There is a merry look in the eyes, and character in the chin.

SIR HARRY (*like an auctioneer*). Noted for her wit.

KATE. All her life before her when that was painted. It is a *spirituelle* face too. (*Suddenly she turns on him with anger, for the first and only time in the play.*) Oh, Harry, you brute !

SIR HARRY (*staggered*). Eh ? What ?

KATE. That dear creature capable of becoming a noble wife and mother—she is the spiritless woman of no account that I saw here a few minutes ago. I forgive you for myself, for I escaped, but that poor lost soul, oh, Harry, Harry.

SIR HARRY (*waving her to the door*). I'll thank you— If ever there was a woman proud of her husband and happy in her married life, that woman is Lady Sims.

KATE. I wonder.

SIR HARRY. Then you needn't wonder.

KATE (*slowly*). If I was a husband—it is my advice to all of them—I would often watch my wife quietly to see whether the twelve-pound look was not coming into her eyes. Two boys, did you say, and both like you?

SIR HARRY. What is that to you?

KATE (*with glistening eyes*). I was only thinking that somewhere there are two little girls who, when they grow up—the dear, pretty girls who are all meant for the men that don't get on! Well, good-bye, Sir Harry.

SIR HARRY (*showing a little human weakness, it is to be feared*). Say first that you're sorry.

KATE. For what?

SIR HARRY. That you left me. Say you

regret it bitterly. You know you do. (*She smiles and shakes her head. He is pettish. He makes a terrible announcement.*) You have spoilt the day for me.

KATE (*to hearten him*). I am sorry for that; but it is only a pin-prick, Harry. I suppose it is a little jarring in the moment of your triumph to find that there is—one old friend —who does not think you a success; but you will soon forget it. Who cares what a typist thinks ?

SIR HARRY (*heartened*). Nobody. A typist at eighteen shillings a week !

KATE (*proudly*). Not a bit of it, Harry. I double that.

SIR HARRY (*neatly*). Magnificent !

(*There is a timid knock at the door.*)

LADY SIMS. May I come in ?

SIR HARRY (*rather appealingly*). It is Lady Sims.

KATE. I won't tell. She is afraid to come into her husband's room without knocking !

SIR HARRY. She is not. (*Uxoriously*) Come in, dearest. (*Dearest enters carrying the sword.*

*She might have had the sense not to bring it in
while this annoying person is here.*)

LADY SIMS (*thinking she has brought her
welcome with her*). Harry, the sword has come.

SIR HARRY (*who will dote on it presently*). Oh,
all right.

LADY SIMS. But I thought you were so
eager to practise with it.

> (*The person smiles at this. He wishes he
> had not looked to see if she was smiling.*)

SIR HARRY (*sharply*). Put it down.

> (LADY SIMS *flushes a little as she lays the
> sword aside.*)

KATE (*with her confounded courtesy*). It is a
beautiful sword, if I may say so.

LADY SIMS (*helped*). Yes.

> (*The person thinks she can put him in the
> wrong, does she? He'll show her.*)

SIR HARRY (*with one eye on* KATE). Emmy,
the one thing your neck needs is more jewels.

LADY SIMS (*faltering*). More!

SIR HARRY. Some ropes of pearls. I'll see
to it. It's a bagatelle to me. (KATE *conceals
her chagrin, so she had better be shown the door.*

He rings.) I won't detain you any longer, miss.

KATE.   Thank you.

LADY SIMS.   Going already ? You have been very quick.

SIR HARRY.   The person doesn't suit, Emmy.

LADY SIMS.   I 'm sorry.

KATE.   So am I, madam, but it can't be helped. Good-bye, your ladyship—good-bye, Sir Harry. (*There is a suspicion of an impertinent curtsy, and she is escorted off the premises by* TOMBES.   *The air of the room is purified by her going.*   SIR HARRY *notices it at once.*)

LADY SIMS (*whose tendency is to say the wrong thing*).   She seemed such a capable woman.

SIR HARRY (*on his hearth*).   I don't like her style at all.

LADY SIMS (*meekly*).   Of course you know best.   (*This is the right kind of woman.*)

SIR HARRY (*rather anxious for corroboration*). Lord, how she winced when I said I was to give you those ropes of pearls.

LADY SIMS.   Did she ? I didn't notice. I suppose so.

SIR HARRY (*frowning*). Suppose ? Surely I know enough about women to know that.

LADY SIMS. Yes, oh yes.

SIR HARRY. (*Odd that so confident a man should ask this.*) Emmy, I know you well, don't I ? I can read you like a book, eh ?

LADY SIMS (*nervously*). Yes, Harry.

SIR HARRY (*jovially, but with an inquiring eye*). What a different existence yours is from that poor lonely wretch's.

LADY SIMS. Yes, but she has a very contented face.

SIR HARRY (*with a stamp of his foot*). All put on. What ?

LADY SIMS (*timidly*). I didn't say anything.

SIR HARRY (*snapping*). One would think you envied her.

LADY SIMS. Envied ? Oh no—but I thought she looked so alive. It was while she was working the machine.

SIR HARRY. Alive ! That's no life. It is you that are alive. (*Curtly*) I'm busy, Emmy. (*He sits at his writing-table.*)

LADY SIMS (*dutifully*). I'm sorry ; I'll go,

HARRY. (*Inconsequentially*) Are they very expensive?

SIR HARRY. What?

LADY SIMS.   Those machines?

*(When she has gone the possible meaning
of her question startles him. The curtain
hides him from us, but we may be sure
that he will soon be bland again. We
have a comfortable feeling, you and I,
that there is nothing of* HARRY SIMS *in
us.)*

PANTALOON

PANTALOON

*The scene makes believe to be the private home of
Pantaloon and Columbine, though whether they ever
did have a private home is uncertain.*

   *In the English version (and with that alone are we
concerning ourselves) these two were figures in the
harlequinade, which in Victorian days gave a finish
to pantomime as vital as a tail to a dog. Now they are
vanished from the boards; or at best they wander
through the canvas streets, in everybody's way, at heart
afraid of their own policeman, really dead, and waiting,
like the faithful old horse, for some one to push them
over. Here at the theatre is perhaps a scrap of
Columbine's skirt, torn off as she squeezed through
the wings for the last time, or even placed there in-
tentionally by her as a souvenir : Columbine to her
public, a kiss hanging on a nail.*

   *They are very illusive. One has to toss to find out
what was their relation to each other : whether Pantaloon, for instance, was Columbine's father. He
was an old, old urchin of the streets over whom some
fairy wand had been waved, rather carelessly, and this*

43

*makes him a child of art ; now we must all be nice to
children of art, and the nicest thing we can do for
Pantaloon is to bring the penny down heads and
give him a delightful daughter. So Columbine was
Pantaloon's daughter.*

*It would be cruel to her to make her his wife, because
then she could not have a love-affair.*

*The mother is dead, to give the little home a touch
of pathos.*

*We have now proved that Pantaloon and his
daughter did have a home, and as soon as we know
that, we know more. We know, for instance, that as
half a crown seemed almost a competency to them,
their home must have been in a poor locality and con-
veniently small. We know also that the sitting-room
and kitchen combined must have been on the ground
floor. We know it, because in the harlequinade they
were always flying from the policeman or bashing his
helmet, and Pantaloon would have taken ill with a
chamber that was not easily commanded by the policeman on his beat. Even Columbine, we may be sure,
refined as she was and incapable of the pettiest larceny,
liked the homely feeling of dodging the policeman's eye
as she sat at meals. Lastly, we know that directly
opposite the little home was a sausage-shop, the
pleasantest of all sights to Pantaloon, who, next to*

his daughter, loved a sausage. It is being almost too intimate to tell that Columbine hated sausages ; she hated them as a literary hand's daughter might hate manuscripts. But like a loving child she never told her hate, and spent great part of her time toasting sausages to a turn before the fire, and eating her own one bravely when she must, but concealing it in the oddest places when she could.

We should now be able to reconstitute Pantaloon's parlour. It is agreeably stuffy, with two windows and a recess between them, from which one may peep both ways for the policeman. The furniture is in horse-hair, no rents showing, because careful Columbine has covered them with antimacassars. All the chairs (but not the sofa) are as sound of limb as they look except one, and Columbine, who is as light as an air balloon, can sit on this one even with her feet off the floor. Though the time is summer there is a fire burning, so that Pantaloon need never eat his sausages raw, which he might do inadvertently if Columbine did not take them gently from his hand. There is a cosy round table with a waxcloth cover adhering to it like a sticking-plaster, and this table is set for tea. Histrionic dignity is given to the room by a large wicker trunk in which Pantaloon's treasures are packed when he travels by rail, and on it is a printed intima-

tion that he is one of the brightest wits on earth. Columbine could be crushed, concertina-like, into half of this trunk, and it may be that she sometimes travels thus to save her ticket. Between the windows hangs a glass case, such as those at inns wherein Piscator preserves his stuffed pike, but this one contains a poker. It is interesting to note that Pantaloon is sufficiently catholic in his tastes to spare a favourable eye for other arts than his own. There are various paintings on the walls, all of himself, with the exception of a small one of his wife. These represent him not in humorous act but for all time, as, for instance, leaning on a bracket and reading a book, with one finger laid lightly against his nose.

So far our work of reconstitution has been easy, but we now come to the teaser. In all these pictures save one (to be referred to in its proper place) Pantaloon is presented not on the stage but in private life, yet he is garbed and powdered as we know him in the harlequinade. If they are genuine portraits, therefore, they tell us something profoundly odd about the home life of Pantaloon; nothing less than this, that as he was on the stage, so he was off it, clothes, powder, and all; he was not acting a part in the harlequinade, he was merely being himself. It was undoubtedly this strange discovery that set us writing a play about him.

Of course bitter controversy may come of this, for not every one will agree that we are right. It is well known among the cognoscenti *that actors in general are not the same off the stage as on; that they dress for their parts, speak words written for them which they do not necessarily believe, and afterwards wash the whole thing off and then go to clubs and coolly cross their legs. I accept this to be so (though I think it a pity), but Pantaloon was never an actor in their sense; he would have scorned to speak words written for him by any whippersnapper; what he said and did before the footlights were the result of mature conviction and represented his philosophy of life. It is the more easy to believe this of him because we are so anxious to believe it of Columbine. Otherwise she could not wear her pretty skirts in our play, and that would be unbearable.*

If this noble and simple consistency was the mark of Pantaloon and Columbine (as we have now proved up to the hilt), it must have distinguished no less the other members of the harlequinade. There were two others, the Harlequin and the Clown.

In far-back days, when the world was so young that pieces of the original egg-shell still adhered to it, one boy was so desperately poor that he alone of children could not don fancy dress on fair days. Presently the other children were sorry for this drab one, so each of them clipped a little bit off his own clothing and gave it to him. These were sewn together and made into a costume for him, by the jolly little tailors who in our days have quite gone out, and that is why Harlequin has come down to us in patchwork. He was a lovely boy with no brains at all (not that this matters), while the Clown was all brain.

It has been our whim to make Pantaloon and Columbine our chief figures, but we have had to go for them, as it were, to the kitchen; the true head of the harlequinade was the Clown. You could not become a clown by taking thought, you had to be born one. It was just a chance. If the Clown had wished to walk over the others they would have spread themselves on the ground so that he should be able to do it without inconveniencing himself. Any money they had they got from him, and it was usually pennies. If they displeased him he caned them. He had too much power and it brutalised him, as we shall see, but in fairness it should be told that he owed his supremacy entirely to his funniness. The family worshipped funniness, and he was the funniest.

It is not necessary for our play to reconstitute the homes of Harlequin and Clown, but it could be done. Harlequin, as a bachelor with no means but with a secret conviction that he was a gentleman, had a sitting-and-bed combined at the top of a house too near Jermyn Street for his purse. He made up by not eating very much, which was good for his figure. He always carried his wand, which had curious magical qualities, for instance it could make him invisible ; but in the street he seldom asked this of it, having indeed a friendly desire to be looked at. He had delightful manners and an honest heart. The Clown, who, of course, had appearances to keep up, knew the value of a good address, and undoubtedly lived in the Cromwell Road. He smoked cigars with bands round them, and his togs were cut in Savile Row.

Clown and Pantaloon were a garrulous pair, but Columbine and Harlequin never spoke. I don't know whether they were what we call dumb. Perhaps if they had tried to talk with their tongues they could have done so, but they never thought of it. They were such exquisite dancers that they did all their talking with their legs. There is nothing that may be said which they could not express with this leg or that. It is the loveliest of all languages, and as soft as the fall of snow.

When the curtain rises we see Columbine alone in the little house, very happy and gay, for she has no notion that her tragic hour is about to strike. She is dressed

D

precisely as we may have seen her on the stage. It is the pink skirt, the white one being usually kept for Sunday, which is also washing-day; and we almost wish this had been Sunday, just to show Columbine in white at the tub, washing the pink without letting a single soap-sud pop on to the white. She is toasting bread rhythmically by the fire, and hides the toasting-fork as the policeman passes suspiciously outside. Presently she is in a whirl of emotion because she has heard Harlequin's knock. She rushes to the window and hides (they were always hiding), she blows kisses, and in her excitement she is everywhere and nowhere at once, like a kitten that leaps at nothing and stops half-way. She has the short quick steps of a bird on a lawn. Long before we have time to describe her movements she has bobbed out of sight beneath the table to await Harlequin funnily, for we must never forget that they are a funny family. With a whirl of his wand that is itself a dance, Harlequin makes the door fly open. He enters, says the stage direction, but what it means is that somehow he is now in the room. He probably knows that Columbine is beneath the table, as she hides so often and there are so few places in the room to hide in, but he searches for her elsewhere, even in a jug, to her extreme mirth, for of course she is peeping at him. He taps the wicker basket with his wand and the lid flies open. Still no Columbine! He sits dejectedly on a chair by the table, with one foot toward the spot where we last saw her head. This is irresistible. She kisses the foot. She is out from beneath the table now, and he is pursuing her round the room. They are as wayward as leaves in a gale. The cunning fellow pretends he does not want her, and now it is she who is pursuing him. There is something entrancing in his hand. It is a ring. It is the engagement-ring at last! She falters, she blushes, but she snatches at the ring. He tantalises her, holding it beyond her reach, but soon she has pulled down his hand and the ring is on her finger. They are dancing ecstatically when Pantaloon comes in and has to drop his stick because she leaps into his arms. If she were not so flurried she would see that the aged man has brought excitement with him also.

PANTALOON. Ah, Fairy! Fond of her dad, is she? Sweetest little daughter ever an old 'un had. (*He sees* HARLEQUIN *and is genial to him, while* HARLEQUIN *pirouettes a How-d' ye-do.*) You here, Boy; welcome, Boy. (*He is about to remove his hat in the ordinary way, but* HARLE-QUIN, *to save his prospective father-in-law any*

little trouble, waves his wand and the hat goes to
rest on a door-peg. The little service so humbly
tendered pleases PANTALOON, *and he surveys*
HARLEQUIN *with kindly condescension.*) Thank
you, Boy. You are a good fellow, Boy, and
an artist too, in your limited way, not here
(*tapping his head*), not in a brainy way, but
lower down (*thoughtfully, and including* COLUM-
BINE *in his downward survey*). That's where
your personality lies — lower down. (*At the*
noble word personality COLUMBINE *thankfully*
crosses herself, and then indicates that tea is
ready.) Tea, Fairy ? I have such glorious
news ; but I will have a dish of tea first. You
will join us, Boy ? Sit down. (*They sit down*
to tea, the lovers exchanging shy, happy glances,
but soon PANTALOON *rises petulantly.*) Fairy,
there are no sausages ! Tea without a sausage.
I am bitterly disappointed. And on a day, too,
when I have great news. It's almost more
than I can bear. No sausages ! (*He is old*
and is near weeping, but COLUMBINE *indicates*
with her personality that if he does not forgive
her she must droop and die, and soon again he

is a magnanimous father.) Yes, yes, my pet, I
forgive you. You can't abide sausages ; nor
can you, Boy. (*They hide their shamed heads.*)
It's not your fault. Some are born with the
instinct for a sausage, and some have it not.
(*More brightly*) Would you like me to be funny
now, my dear, or shall we have tea first ?
(*They prefer to have tea first, and the courteous
old man sits down with them.*) But you do
think me funny, don't you, Fairy ? Neither
of you can look at me without laughing, can
you ? Try, Boy ; try, Fairy. (*They try, but
fail. He is moved.*) Thank you both, thank
you kindly. If the public only knew how
anxiously we listen for the laugh they would
be less grudging of it. (*Hastily*) Not that
I have any cause of complaint. Every night
I get the laugh from my generous patrons,
the public, and always by legitimate means.
When I think what a favourite I am I cannot
keep my seat. (*He rises proudly.*) I am
acknowledged by all in the know to be a funny
old man. (*He moves about exultantly, looking
at the portraits that are to hand him down to*

posterity.) That picture of me, Boy, was
painted to commemorate my being the second
funniest man on earth. Of course Joey is the
funniest, but I am the second funniest. (*They
have scarcely listened ; they have been exchanging delicious glances with face and foot. But at
mention of the* CLOWN *they shudder a little, and
their hands seek each other for protection*.) This
portrait I had took—done—in honour of your
birth, my love. I call it ' The Old 'Un on First
Hearing that He is a Father.' (*He chuckles
long before another picture which represents him
in the dress of ordinary people*.) This is me in
fancy dress ; it is how I went to a fancy-dress
ball. Your mother, Fairy, was with me, in a
long skirt ! Very droll we must have looked, and
very droll we felt. I call to mind we walked
about in this way ; the way the public walks,
you know. (*In his gaiety he imitates the walk
of the public, and roguish* COLUMBINE *imitates
them also, but she loses her balance*.) Yes, try it.
Don't flutter so much. Ah, it won't do, Fairy.
Your natural way of walking 's like a bird
bobbing about on a lawn after worms. Your

mother was the same, and when she got low in spirits I just blew her about the room till she was lively again. Blow Fairy about, Boy. (HARLEQUIN *blows her divinely about the room, against the wall, on to seats and off them, and for some sad happy moments* PANTALOON *gazes at her, feeling that his wife is alive again. They think it is the auspicious time to tell him of their love, but bashfulness falls upon them. He only sees that their faces shine.*) Ah, she is happy, my Fairy, but I have news that will make her happier! (*Curiously*) Fairy, you look as if you had something you wanted to tell me. Have you news too? (*Tremblingly she extends her hand and shows him the ring on it. For a moment he misunderstands.*) A ring! Did *he* give you that? (*She nods rapturously.*) Oho, oho, this makes me so happy. I 'll be funnier than ever, if possible. (*At this they dance glee-fully, but his next words strike them cold.*) But, the rogue! He said he wanted me to speak to you about it first. That was my news. Oh, the rogue! (*They are scared, and sudden fear grips him.*) There 's nothing wrong, is there?

It was Joey gave you that ring, wasn't it, Fairy ? (*She shakes her head, and the movement shakes tears from her eyes.*) If it wasn't Joey, who was it ? (HARLEQUIN *steps forward.*) You ! You are not fond of Boy, are you, Fairy ? (*She is clinging to her lover now, and* PANTALOON *is a little dazed.*) But, my girl, Joey wants you. A clown wants you. When a clown wants you, you are not going to fling yourself away on a harlequin, are you ? (*They go on their knees to him, and he is touched, but also frightened.*) Don't try to get round me ; now don't. Joey would be angry with me. He can be hard when he likes, Joey can. (*In a whisper*) Perhaps he would cane me ! You wouldn't like to see your dad caned, Fairy. (COLUMBINE'S *head sinks to the floor in woe, and* HARLEQUIN *eagerly waves his wand.*) Ah, Boy, you couldn't defy him. He is our head. You can do wonderful things with that wand, but you can't fight Joey with it. (*Sadly enough the wand is lowered.*) You see, children, it won't do. You have no money, Boy, except the coppers Joey sometimes gives you in an envelope of a Friday night, and we can't marry without money (*with an attempt at joviality*), can't marry without money, Boy. (HARLEQUIN *with a rising chest produces money.*) Seven shillings and tenpence! You have been saving up, Boy. Well done! But it's not enough. (COLUMBINE *darts to the mantelshelf for her money-box and rattles it triumphantly.* PANTALOON *looks inside it.*) A half-crown and two sixpences! It won't do, children. I had a pound and a piano-case when I married, and yet I was pinched. (*They sit on the floor with their fingers to their eyes, and with difficulty he restrains an impulse to sit beside them.*) Poor souls! poor true love! (*The thought of Joey's power and greatness overwhelms him.*) Think of Joey's individuality, Fairy. He banks his money, my love. If you saw the boldness of Joey in the bank when he hands the slip across the counter and counts his money, my pet, instead of being thankful for whatever they give him. And then he puts out his tongue at them! The artist in him makes him put out his tongue at them. For he is a great

artist, Joey. He is a greater artist than I am.
I know it and I admit it. He has a touch
that is beyond me. (*Imploringly*) Did you
say you would marry him, my love ? (*She does
not raise her head, and he continues with a new
break in his voice.*) It is not his caning me I
am so afraid of, but—but I 'm oldish now,
Fairy, even for an old 'un, and there is something
I must tell you. I have tried to keep it from
myself, but I know. It is this : I am afraid,
my sweet, I am not so funny as I used to be.
(*She encircles his knees in dissent.*) Yes, it 's
true, and Joey knows it. On Monday I had
to fall into the barrel three times before I got
the laugh. Joey saw ! If Joey were to dismiss
me I could never get another shop. I would
be like a dog without a master. He has been
my master so long. I have put by nearly
enough to keep me, but oh, Fairy, the awful-
ness of not being famous any longer. Living
on without seeing my kind friends in front.
To think of my just being one of the public,
of my being pointed at in the streets as the
old 'un that was fired out of the company

because he missed his laughs. And that 's what
Joey will bring to pass if you don't marry
him, my girl. (*It is an appeal for mercy, and*
COLUMBINE *is his loving daughter. Her face is*
wan, but she tries to smile. She hugs the ring to
her breast, and then gives it back to HARLEQUIN.
They try to dance a last embrace, but their legs
are leaden. He kisses her cheeks and her foot
and goes away broken-hearted. The brave girl
puts her arm round her father's neck and hides
her wet face. He could not look at it though it
were exposed, for he has more to tell.) I haven't
told you the worst yet, my love. I didn't dare
tell you the worst till Boy had gone. Fairy,
the marriage is to be to-day! Joey has
arranged it all. It 's his humour, and we dare
not thwart him. He is coming here to take
you to the wedding. (*In a tremble she draws*
away from him.) I haven't been a bad father
to you, have I, my girl? When we were waiting for you before you were born, your mother
and I, we used to wonder what you would be
like, and I—it was natural, for I was always
an ambitious man—I hoped you would be a

clown. But that wasn't to be, and when the
doctor came to me—I was walking up and down
this room in a tremble, for my darling was
always delicate—when the doctor came to me
and said, ' I congratulate you, sir, on being the
father of a fine little columbine,' I never uttered
one word of reproach to him or to you or to
her. (*There is a certain grandeur about the old
man as he calls attention to the nobility of his
conduct, but it falls from him on the approach of
the* CLOWN. *We hear Joey before we see him:
he is singing a snatch of one of his triumphant
ditties, less for his own pleasure perhaps than to
warn the policeman to be on the alert. He has
probably driven to the end of the street, and then
walked. A tremor runs through* COLUMBINE *at
sound of him, but* PANTALOON *smiles, a foolish
ecstatic smile. Joey has always been his hero.*)
Be ready to laugh, my girl. Joey will be angry
if he doesn't get the laugh.

　　　　(*The* CLOWN *struts in, as confident of
　　　　welcome as if he were the announcement
　　　　of dinner. He wears his motley like an
　　　　order. A silk hat and an eyeglass indi-*

cate his superior social position. A sausage protruding from a pocket shows that he can unbend at times. A masterful man when you don't applaud enough, he is at present in uproarious spirits, as if he had just looked in a mirror. At first he affects not to see his host, to PANTALOON'S *great entertainment.*)

CLOWN. Miaw, miaw !

PANTALOON (*bent with merriment*). He is at his funniest, quite at his funniest.

(CLOWN *kicks him hard but good-naturedly, and* PANTALOON *falls to the ground.*)

CLOWN. Miaw !

PANTALOON (*reverently*). What an artist.

CLOWN (*pretends to see* COLUMBINE *for the first time in his life. In a masterpiece of funniness he starts back, like one dazzled by a naked light*). Oh, Jiminy Crinkles ! Oh, I say, what a beauty.

PANTALOON. There's nobody like him.

CLOWN. It's Fairy. It's my little Fairy.

(*Strange, but all her admiration for this man has gone. He represents nothing to*

*her now but wealth and social rank. He
ogles her, and she shrinks from him as if
he were something nauseous.*)

PANTALOON (*warningly*). Fairy !

CLOWN (*showing sharp teeth*). Hey, what's
this, old 'un ? Don't she admire me ?

PANTALOON. Not admire you, Joey ? That's
a good 'un. Joey's at his best to-day.

CLOWN. Ain't she ready to come to her
wedding ?

PANTALOON. She's ready, Joey.

CLOWN (*producing a cane, and lowering*).
Have you told her what will happen to you if
she ain't ready ?

PANTALOON (*backing*). I've told her, Joey
(*supplicating*). Get your hat, Fairy.

CLOWN. Why ain't she dancing wi' joy and
pride ?

PANTALOON. She is, Joey, she is.

(COLUMBINE *attempts to dance with joy
and pride, and the* CLOWN *has been so
long used to adulation that he is deceived.*)

CLOWN (*amiable again*). Parson's waiting.
Oh. what a lark.

PANTALOON (*with a feeling that lark is not perhaps the happiest word for the occasion*). Get your things, Fairy.

CLOWN (*riding on a chair*). Give me something first, my lovey-dovey. I shuts my eyes and opens my mouth, and waits for what's my doo. (*She knows what he means, and it is sacrilege to her. But her father's arms are extended beseechingly. She gives the now abhorred countenance a kiss, and runs from the room. The* CLOWN *plays with the kiss as if it were a sausage, a sight abhorrent to* HARLEQUIN, *who has stolen in by the window. Fain would he strike, but though he is wearing his mask, which is a sign that he is invisible, he fears to do so. As if conscious of the unseen presence, the* CLOWN's *brow darkens.*) Joey, when I came in I saw Boy hanging around outside.

PANTALOON (*ill at ease*). Boy? What can he be wanting?

CLOWN. I know what he is wanting, and I know what he will get. (*He brandishes the cane threateningly. At the same moment the wedding bells begin to peal.*)

PANTALOON. Hark!

CLOWN (*with grotesque accompaniment*). My wedding bells. Fairy's wedding bells. There they go again, here we are again, there they go again, here we are again. (COLUMBINE *returns. She has tried to hide the tears on her cheeks behind a muslin veil. There is a melancholy bouquet in her hand. She passionately desires to be like the respectable public on her marriage day.* HARLEQUIN *raises his mask for a moment that she may see him, and they look long at each other, those two, who are never to have anything lovely to look at again.* 'Won't he save her yet?' *says her face, but* 'I am afraid' *says his. Still the bells are jangling.*)

PANTALOON. My girl.

CLOWN. Mine. (*He kisses her, but it is the sausage look that is in his eyes.* PANTALOON, *bleeding for his girl, raises his staff to strike him, but* COLUMBINE *will not have the sacrifice. She gives her arm to the* CLOWN.) To the wedding. To the wedding. Old 'un, lead on, and we will follow thee! Oh, what a lark!

(*They are going toward the door, but in*

this supreme moment love turns timid Boy into a man. He waves his mysterious wand over them, so that all three are suddenly bereft of movement. They are like frozen figures. He removes his mask and smiles at them with a terrible face. Fondly and leisurely he gathers COLUMBINE *in his arms and carries her out by the window. The* CLOWN *and* PANTALOON *remain there, as if struck in the act of taking a step forward. The wedding bells are still pealing.)*

The curtain falls for a moment only. It rises on the same room several years later.

The same room; as one may say of a suit of clothes, out of which the whilom tenant has long departed, that they are the same man. A room cold to the touch, dilapidated, fragments of the ceiling fallen and left where they fell, wall-paper peeling damply, portraits of PANTALOON *taken down to sell, unsaleable, and never rehung. Once such a clean room that its*

E

ghost to-day might be COLUMBINE *chasing a speck of dust, it is now untended. Even the windows are grimy, which tells a tale of* PANTALOON'S *final capitulation; while any heart was left him we may be sure he kept the windows clean so that the police-man might spy upon him. Perhaps the policeman has gone from the street, bored, nothing doing there now.*

It is evening and winter time, and the ancient man is moving listlessly about his room, mechanically blowing life into his hands as if he had forgotten that there is no real reason why there should be life in them. The clothes COLUMBINE *used to brush with such care are slovenly, the hair she so often smoothed with all her love is unkempt. He is smaller, a man who has shrunk into himself in shame, not so much shame that he is uncared for as that he is forgotten.*

He is sitting forlorn by the fire when the door opens to admit his first visitor for years. It is the CLOWN, *just sufficiently*

*stouter to look more resplendent. The
drum, so to say, is larger. He gloats over
the bowed* PANTALOON *like a spiteful
boy.*

CLOWN (*poking* PANTALOON *with his cane*).
Who can this miserable ancient man be ?

(*Visited at last by some one who knows
him,* PANTALOON *rises in a surge of joy.*)

PANTALOON. You have come back, Joey,
after all these years !

CLOWN. Hands off. I came here, my good
fellow, to inquire for a Mr. Joseph.

PANTALOON (*shuddering*). Yes, that's me ;
that's all that's left of me ; Mr. Joseph ! Me
that used to be Joey.

CLOWN. I think I knew you once, Mr.
Joseph ?

PANTALOON. Joey, you're hard on me. It
wasn't my fault that Boy tricked us and ran
off wi' her.

CLOWN. May I ask, Mr. Joseph, were you
ever on the boards ?

PANTALOON. This to me as was your right
hand !

CLOWN. I seem to call to mind something like you as used to play the swell.

PANTALOON (*fiercely*). It's a lie! I was born a Pantaloon, and a Pantaloon I'll die.

CLOWN. Yes, I heard you was dead, Mr. Joseph. Everybody knows it except yourself. (*He gnaws a sausage.*)

PANTALOON (*greedily*). Gie me a bite, Joey.

CLOWN (*relentless*). I only bites with the profession. I never bites with the public.

PANTALOON. What brought you here? Just to rub it in?

CLOWN. Let's say I came to make inquiries after the happy pair.

PANTALOON. It's years and years, Joey, since they ran away, and I've never seen them since.

CLOWN. Heard of them?

PANTALOON. Yes, I've heard. They're in distant parts.

CLOWN. Answer their letters?

PANTALOON (*darkening*). No.

CLOWN. They will be doing well, Mr. Joseph, without me?

PANTALOON (*boastfully*). At first they did badly, but when the managers heard Fairy was my daughter they said the daughter o' such a famous old 'un was sure to draw by reason of her father's name. And they print the name of her father in big letters.

CLOWN (*rapping it out*). It's you that lie now. I know about them. They go starving like vagabonds from town to town.

PANTALOON. Ay, it's true. They write that they're starving.

CLOWN. And they've got a kid to add to their misery. All vagabonds, father, mother, and kid.

PANTALOON. Rub it in, Joey.

CLOWN. You looks as if you would soon be starving too.

PANTALOON (*not without dignity*). I'm pinched.

CLOWN. Well, well, I'm a kindly soul, and what brought me here was to make you an offer.

PANTALOON (*glistening*). A shop?

CLOWN. For old times' sake.

PANTALOON (*with indecent eagerness*). To be old 'un again ?

CLOWN. No, you crock, but to carry a sandwich-board in the street wi' my new old 'un's name on it.

> (PANTALOON *raises his withered arm, but he lets it fall.*)

PANTALOON. May you be forgiven for that, Joey.

CLOWN. Miaw !

PANTALOON (*who is near his end*). Joey, there stands humbled before you an old artist.

CLOWN. Never an artist.

PANTALOON (*firmly*). An artist—at present disengaged.

CLOWN. Forgotten—clean forgotten.

PANTALOON (*bowing his head*). Yes, that's it—forgotten. Once famous—now forgotten. Joey, they don't know me even at the sausage-shop. I am just one of the public. My worst time is when we should be going on the stage, and I think I hear the gallery boys calling for the old 'un—' Bravo, old 'un ! ' Then I sort of break up. I sleep bad o' nights. I think sleep would come to me if I could rub my back on the scenery again. (*He shudders.*) But the days are longer than the nights. I allus see how I am to get through to-day, but I sit thinking and thinking how I am to get through to-morrow.

CLOWN. Poor old crock. Well, so long.

PANTALOON (*offering him the poker*). Joey, gie me one rub before you go—for old times' sake.

CLOWN. You 'll never be rubbed by a clown again, Mr. Joseph.

PANTALOON. Call me Joey once—say ' Goodbye, old 'un'—for old times' sake.

CLOWN. You will never be called Joey or old 'un by a clown again, Mr. Joseph.

> (*With a noble gesture* PANTALOON *bids him begone and the* CLOWN *miaws and goes, twisting a sausage in his mouth as if it were a cigar. So he passes from our sight, funny to the last, or never funny, an equally tragic figure.*
>
> PANTALOON *rummages in the wicker basket among his gods and strokes them*

lovingly, a painted goose, his famous staff, a bladder on a stick. He does not know that he is hugging the bladder to his cold breast as he again crouches by the fire.

The door opens, and COLUMBINE *and* HARLEQUIN *peep in, prepared to receive a blow for welcome. Their faces are hollow and their clothes in rags, and, saddest of all, they cannot dance in. They walk in like the weary public.* COLUMBINE *looks as if she could walk as far as her father's feet, but never any farther. With them is the child. This is the great surprise:* HE IS A CLOWN. *They sign to the child to intercede for them, but though only a baby, he is a clown, and he must do it in his own way. He pats his nose, grins deliciously with the wrong parts of his face, and dives beneath the table.* PANTALOON *looks round and sees his daughter on her knees before him.*)

PANTALOON. You! Fairy! Come back! (*For a moment he is to draw her to him, then he remembers.*) No, I'll have none of you. It was you as brought me to this. Begone, I say begone. (*They are backing meekly to the door.*) Stop a minute. Little Fairy, is it true—is it true my Fairy has a kid? (*She nods, with glistening eyes that say 'Can you put me out now?' The baby peers from under the table, and rubs* PANTALOON'S *legs with the poker. Poor little baby, he is the last of the clowns, and knows not what is in store for him.* PANTALOON *trembles, it is so long since he has been rubbed. He dare not look down.*) Fairy, is it the kid? (*She nods again; the moment has come.*) My Fairy's kid! (*Somehow he has always taken for granted that his grandchild is merely a columbine. If the child had been something greater they would all have got a shop again and served under him.*) Oh, Fairy, if only he had been a clown!

> (*Now you see how it is going. The babe emerges, and he is a clown.*
>
> *Just for a moment* PANTALOON *cries. Then the babe is tantalising him with a sausage.* PANTALOON *revolves round him*

*like a happy teetotum. Who so gay now
as* COLUMBINE *and* HARLEQUIN, *dancing
merrily as if it were again the morning?
Oh what a lark is life. Ring down the
curtain quickly, Mr. Prompter, before we
see them all swept into the dust-heap.*)

ROSALIND

ROSALIND

ROSALIND

*Two middle-aged ladies are drinking tea in the parlour
of a cottage by the sea. It is far from London, and a
hundred yards from the cry of children, of whom
middle-aged ladies have often had enough. Were
the room Mrs. Page's we should make a journey
through it in search of character, but she is only a bird
of passage; nothing of herself here that has not
strayed from her bedroom except some cushions and
rugs: touches of character after all maybe, for they
suggest that Mrs. Page likes to sit soft.*

*The exterior of the cottage is probably picturesque,
with a thatched roof, but we shall never know for certain,
it being against the rules of the game to step outside
and look. The old bowed window of the parlour is of
the engaging kind that still brings some carriage folk
to a sudden stop in villages, not necessarily to sample
the sweets of yester-year exposed within in bottles;
its panes are leaded; but Mrs. Quickly will put
something more modern in their place if ever her ship
comes home. They will then be used as the roof of*

the hencoop, and ultimately some lovely lady, given, like the chickens, to 'picking up things,' may survey the world through them from a window in Mayfair. The parlour is, by accident, like some woman's face that scores by being out of drawing. At present the window is her smile, but one cannot fix features to the haphazard floor, nor to the irregular walls, which nevertheless are part of the invitation to come and stay here. There are two absurd steps leading up to Mrs. Page's bedroom, and perhaps they are what give the room its retroussée touch. There is a smell of seaweed; twice a day Neptune comes gallantly to the window and hands Mrs. Page the smell of seaweed. He knows probably that she does not like to have to go far for her seaweed. Perhaps he also suspects her to be something of a spark, and looks forward to his evening visits, of which we know nothing.

This is a mere suggestion that there may be more in Mrs. Page (when the moon is up, say) than meets the eye, but we see at present only what does meet the eye as she gossips with her landlady at the tea-table. Is she good-looking? is the universal shriek; the one question on the one subject that really thrills humanity. But the question seems beside the point about this particular lady, who has so obviously ceased to have any interest in the answer. To us who have a few moments to sum her up while she is still at the tea-table (just time enough for sharp ones to form a wrong impression), she is an indolent, sloppy thing, this Mrs. Page of London, decidedly too plump, and averse to pulling the strings that might contract her ; as Mrs. Quickly may have said, she has let her figure go and snapped her fingers at it as it went. Her hair is braided back at a minimum of labour (and the brush has been left on the parlour mantel-piece). She wears at tea-time a loose and dowdy dressing-gown and large flat slippers. Such a lazy woman (shall we venture ?) that if she were a beggar and you offered her alms, she would ask you to put them in her pocket for her.

Yet we notice, as contrary to her type, that she is not only dowdy but self-consciously enamoured of her dowdiness, has a kiss for it so to speak. This is odd, and perhaps we had better have another look at her. The thing waggling gaily beneath the table is one of her feet, from which the sprawling slipper has dropped, to remain where it fell. It is an uncommonly pretty foot, and one instantly wonders what might not the rest of her be like if it also escaped from its moorings.

The foot returns into custody, without its owner having to stoop, and Mrs. Page crosses with cheerful languor to a chair by the fire. She has a drawling walk that fits her gown. There is no footstool within reach, and she pulls another chair to her with her feet and rests them on it contentedly. The slippers almost hide her from our view.

DAME QUICKLY. You Mrs. Cosy Comfort.

MRS. PAGE (*whose voice is as lazy as her walk*). That's what I am. Perhaps a still better name for me would be Mrs. Treacly Content-ment. Dame, you like me, don't you? Come here, and tell me why.

DAME. What do I like you for, Mrs. Page? Well, for one thing, it's very kind of you to let me sit here drinking tea and gossiping with you, for all the world as if I were your equal. And for another, you always pay your book the day I bring it to you, and that is enough to make any poor woman like her lodger.

MRS. PAGE. Oh, as a lodger I know I'm well enough, and I love our gossips over the teapot, but that is not exactly what I meant. Let me put it in this way : If you tell me what you most envy in me, I shall tell you what I most envy in you.

DAME (*with no need to reflect*). Well, most of all, ma'am, I think I envy you your contentment with middle-age.

MRS. PAGE (*purring*). I am middle-aged, so why should I complain of it ?

DAME (*who feels that only yesterday she was driving the youths to desperation*). You even say it as if it were a pretty word.

MRS. PAGE. But isn't it ?

DAME. Not when you are up to the knees in it, as I am.

MRS. PAGE. And as I am. But I dote on it. It is such a comfy, sloppy, pull-the-curtains, carpet-slipper sort of word. When I awake in the morning, Dame, and am about to leap out of bed like the girl I once was, I suddenly remember, and I cry ' Hurrah, I 'm middle-aged.'

DAME. You just dumbfounder me when you tell me things like that. (*Here is something she has long wanted to ask.*) You can't be more than forty, if I may make so bold ?

MRS. PAGE. I am forty and a bittock, as the Scotch say. That means forty, and a good wee bit more.

F

DAME.   There !   And you can say it without blinking.

MRS. PAGE.   Why not ?   Do you think I should call myself a 30-to-45, like a motor-car ? Now what I think I envy you for most is for being a grandmamma.

DAME (*smiling tolerantly at some picture the words have called up*).   That 's a cheap honour.

MRS. PAGE (*summing up probably her whole conception of the duties of a grandmother*).   I should love to be a grandmamma, and toss little toddlekins in the air.

DAME (*who knows that there is more in it than that*).   I dare say you will be some day.

> (*The eyes of both turn to a photograph on the mantelpiece. It represents a pretty woman in the dress of Rosalind. The* DAME *fingers it for the hundredth time, and* MRS. PAGE *regards her tranquilly.*)

DAME.   No one can deny but your daughter is a pretty piece.   How old will she be now ?

MRS. PAGE.   Dame, I don't know very much about the stage, but I do know that you should never, never ask an actress's age.

DAME.　Surely when they are as young and famous as this puss is.

MRS. PAGE.　She is getting on, you know. Shall we say twenty-three ?

DAME.　Well, well, it's true you might be a grandmother by now.　I wonder she doesn't marry.　Where is she now ?

MRS. PAGE.　At Monte Carlo, the papers say. It is a place where people gamble.

DAME (*shaking her head*).　Gamble ?　Dear, dear, that's terrible.　(*But she knows of a woman who once won a dinner service without anything untoward happening afterwards*.)　And yet I would like just once to put on my shilling with the best of them.　If I were you I would try a month of that place with her.

MRS. PAGE.　Not I, I am just Mrs. Cosy Comfort.　At Monte Carlo I should be a fish out of water, Dame, as much as Beatrice would be if she were to try a month down here with me.

DAME (*less in disparagement of local society than of that sullen bore the sea, and blissfully unaware that it intrudes even at Monte Carlo*).　Yes,

I 'm thinking she would find this a dull hole. (*In the spirit of adventure that has carried the English far*) And yet, play-actress though she be, I would like to see her, God forgive me.

> (*She is trimming the lamp when there is a knock at the door. She is pleasantly flustered, and indicates with a gesture that something is constantly happening in this go-ahead village.*)

DAME. It has a visitor's sound.

> (*The lodger is so impressed that she takes her feet off the chair. Thus may* MRS. QUICKLY'S *ancestors have stared at each other in this very cottage a hundred years ago when they thought they heard Napoleon tapping.*)

MRS. PAGE (*keeping her head*). If it is the doctor's lady, she wants to arrange with me about the cutting out for the mothers' meeting.

DAME (*who has long ceased to benefit from these gatherings*). Drat the mothers' meetings.

MRS. PAGE. Oh no, I dote on them. (*She is splendidly active; in short, the spirited woman has got up.*)   Still, I want my evening snooze now, so just tell her I am lying down.

DAME (*thankful to be in a plot*).   I will.

MRS. PAGE.   Yes, but let me lie down first, so that it won't be a fib.

DAME.   There, there.   That 's such a middle-aged thing to say.

> (*In the most middle-aged way* MRS. PAGE *spreads herself on a couch.   They have been speaking in a whisper, and as the* DAME *goes to the door we have just time to take note that* MRS. PAGE *whispered most beautifully :   a softer whisper than the* DAME'S, *but so clear that it might be heard across a field.   This is the most tell-tale thing we have discovered about her as yet.*

> *Before* MRS. QUICKLY *has reached the door it opens to admit an impatient young man in knickerbockers and a Norfolk jacket, all aglow with raindrops.   Public school (and the particular one) is written on his forehead, and almost nothing else ; he has scarcely yet begun to surmise that anything else may be required.   He is modest and*

*clear-eyed, and would ring for his tub in
Paradise ; reputably athletic also, with an
instant smile always in reserve for the
antagonist who accidentally shins him.
Whatever you, as his host, ask him to do,
he says he would like to awfully if you don't
mind his being a priceless duffer at it ;
his vocabulary is scanty, and in his engaging mouth ' priceless' sums up all that is
to be known of good or ill in our varied
existence ; at a pinch it would suffice him
for most of his simple wants, just as one
may traverse the Continent with* Combien ?
*His brain is quite as good as another's, but
as yet he has referred scarcely anything to
it.   He respects learning in the aged, but
shrinks uncomfortably from it in contem-
poraries, as persons who have somehow
failed.   To him the proper way to look
upon ability is as something we must all
come to in the end.   He has a nice taste in
the arts that has come to him by the way of
socks, spats and slips, and of these he has
a large and happy collection, which he*

laughs at jollily in public (for his sense of humour is sufficient), but in the privacy of his chamber he sometimes spreads them out like troutlet on the river's bank and has his quiet thrills of exultation. Having lately left Oxford, he is facing the world confidently with nothing to impress it except these and his Fives Choice (having beaten Hon. Billy Minhorn in the final). He has not yet decided whether to drop into business or diplomacy or the bar. (There will be a lot of fag about this) ; and all unknown to him there is a grim piece of waste land waiting for him in Canada, which he will make a hash of, or it will make a man of him. Billy will be there too.)

CHARLES (*on the threshold*). I beg your pardon awfully, but I knocked three times.

DAME (*liking the manner of him, and indeed it is the nicest manner in the world*). What's your pleasure ?

CHARLES. You see how jolly wet my things are. (*These boys get on delightful terms of intimacy at once.*) I am on a walking tour—not

that I have walked much—(*they never boast;
he has really walked well and far*)—and I got
caught in that shower. I thought when I saw
a house that you might be kind enough to let
me take my jacket off and warm my paws, until
I can catch a train.

DAME (*unable to whisper to* MRS. PAGE '*He is
good-looking*'). I'm sorry, sir, but I have let
the kitchen fire out.

CHARLES (*peeping over her shoulder*). This
fire—— ?

DAME. This is my lodger's room.

CHARLES. Ah, I see. Still, I dare say that
if he knew—— (*He has edged farther into the
room, and becomes aware that there is a lady with
eyes closed on the sofa.*) I beg your pardon ;
I didn't know there was any one here.

> (*But the lady on the sofa replies not, and to
> the* DAME *this is his dismissal.*)

DAME. The station is just round the corner,
and there is a waiting-room there.

CHARLES. A station waiting-room fire ; I
know them. Is she asleep ?

DAME. Yes.

CHARLES (*who nearly always gets round them when he pouts*). Then can't I stay? I won't disturb her.

DAME (*obdurate*). I'm sorry.

CHARLES (*cheerily—he will probably do well on that fruit-farm*). Heigho! Well, here is for the station waiting-room.

> (*And he is about to go when* MRS. PAGE *signs to the* DAME *that he may stay. We have given the talk between the* DAME *and* CHARLES *in order to get it over, but our sterner eye is all the time on* MRS. PAGE. *Her eyes remain closed as if in sleep and she is lying on the sofa, yet for the first time since the curtain rose she has come to life. As if she knew we were watching her she is again inert, but there was a twitch of the mouth a moment ago that let a sunbeam loose upon her face. It is gone already, popped out of the box and returned to it with the speed of thought. Noticeable as is* MRS. PAGE'S *mischievous smile, far more noticeable is her control of it. A sudden thought occurs to us that the*

face we had thought stolid is made of elastic.)

DAME (*cleverly*). After all, if you 're willing just to sit quietly by the fire and take a book——

CHARLES. Rather. Any book. Thank you immensely. (*And in his delightful way of making himself at home he whips off his knapsack and steps inside the fender. ' He is saucy, thank goodness,' is what the DAME's glance at MRS. PAGE conveys. That lady's eyelids flicker as if she had discovered a way of watching CHARLES while she slumbers. Anon his eye alights on the photograph that has already been the subject of conversation, and he is instantly exclamatory.*)

DAME (*warningly*). Now, you promised not to speak.

CHARLES. But that photograph. How funny you should have it.

DAME (*severely*). Hsh. It 's not mine.

CHARLES (*with his first glance of interest at the sleeper*). Hers ?

> (*The eyelids have ceased to flicker. It is placid* MRS. PAGE *again. Never was such an inelastic face.*)

DAME. Yes; only don't talk.

CHARLES. But this is priceless (*gazing at the photograph*). I must talk. (*He gives his reason.*) I know her (*a reason that would be complimentary to any young lady*). It is Miss Beatrice Page.

DAME (*who knows the creature man*). You mean you 've seen her?

CHARLES (*youthfully*). I know her quite well. I have had lunch with her twice. She is at Monte Carlo just now. (*Swelling*) I was one of those that saw her off.

DAME. Yes, that 's the place. Read what is written across her velvet chest.

CHARLES (*deciphering the writing on the photograph*). 'To darling Mumsy with heaps of kisses.' (*His eyes gleam. Is he in the middle of an astonishing adventure?*) You don't tell me— Is that——?

DAME (*as coolly as though she were passing the butter*). Yes, that 's her mother. And a sore trial it must have been to her when her girl took to such a trade.

CHARLES (*waving aside such nonsense*). But I say, she never spoke to me about a mother.

DAME. The more shame to her.

CHARLES (*deeply versed in the traffic of the stage*). I mean she is famed as being almost the only actress who doesn't have a mother.

DAME (*bewildered*). What?

CHARLES (*seeing the uselessness of laying pearls before this lady*). Let me have a look at her.

DAME. It is not to be thought of. (*But an unexpected nod from the sleeper indicates that it may be permitted.*) Oh, well, I see no harm in it if you go softly.

> (*He tiptoes to the sofa, but perhaps* MRS. PAGE *is a light sleeper, for she stirs a little, just sufficiently to become more compact, while the slippers rise into startling prominence. Some humorous dream, as it might be, slightly extends her mouth and turns the oval of her face into a round. Her head has sunk into her neck. Simultaneously, as if her circulation were suddenly held up, a shadow passes over her complexion. This is a bad copy of the* MRS. PAGE *we have seen hitherto, and will give* CHARLES *a poor impression of her.*)

CHARLES (*peering over the slippers*). Yes, yes, yes.

DAME. Is she like the daughter, think you?

CHARLES (*judicially*). In a way, very. Hair's not so pretty. She's not such a fine colour. Heavier build, and I should say not so tall. None of Miss Page's distinction, nothing *svelte* about her. As for the feet (*he might almost have said the palisade*)—the feet—— (*He shudders a little, and so do the feet.*)

DAME. She is getting on, you see. She is forty and a bittock.

CHARLES. A whattock?

DAME (*who has never studied the Doric*). It may be a whattock.

CHARLES (*gallantly*). But there's something nice about her. I could have told she was her mother anywhere. (*With which handsome compliment he returns to the fire, and* MRS. PAGE, *no doubt much gratified, throws a kiss after him. She also signs to the* DAME *a mischievous desire to be left alone with this blade.*)

DAME (*discreetly*). Well, I'll leave you, but, mind, you are not to disturb her.

(*She goes, with the pleasant feeling that there are two clever women in the house; and with wide-open eyes* MRS. PAGE *watches* CHARLES *dealing amorously with the photograph. Soon he returns to her side, and her eyes are closed, but she does not trouble to repeat the trifling with her appearance. She probably knows the strength of first impressions.*)

CHARLES (*murmuring the word as if it were sweet music*). Mumsy. (*With conviction*) You lucky mother.

MRS. PAGE (*in a dream*). Is that you, Beatrice?

(*This makes him skurry away, but he is soon back again, and the soundness of her slumber annoys him.*)

CHARLES (*in a reproachful whisper*). Woman, wake up and talk to me about your daughter.

(*The selfish thing sleeps on, and somewhat gingerly he pulls away the cushion from beneath her head. Nice treatment for a lady.* MRS. PAGE *starts up, and at first is not quite sure where she is, you know.*)

MRS. PAGE. Why—what——

CHARLES (*contritely*). I am very sorry. I'm afraid I disturbed you.

MRS. PAGE (*blankly*). I don't know you, do I?

CHARLES (*who has his inspirations*). No, madam, but I wish you did.

MRS. PAGE (*making sure that she is still in the* DAME'S *cottage*). Who are you? and what are you doing here?

CHARLES (*for truth is best*). My name is Roche. I am nobody in particular. I'm just the usual thing; Eton, Oxford, and so to bed— as Pepys would say. I am on a walking tour, on my way to the station, but there is no train till seven, and your landlady let me in out of the rain on the promise that I wouldn't disturb you.

MRS. PAGE (*taking it all in with a woman's quickness*). I see. (*Suddenly*) But you have disturbed me.

CHARLES. I'm sorry.

MRS. PAGE (*with a covert eye on him*). It wasn't really your fault. This cushion slipped from under me, and I woke up.

CHARLES (*manfully*).   No, I—I pulled it away.

MRS. PAGE (*indignant*).   You did! (*She advances upon him like a stately ship.*)   Will you please to tell me why?

CHARLES (*feebly*).   I didn't mean to pull so hard.   (*Then he gallantly leaps into the breach.*) Madam, I felt it was impossible for me to leave this house without first waking you to tell you of the feelings of solemn respect with which I regard you.

MRS. PAGE.   Really.

CHARLES.   I suppose I consider you the cleverest woman in the world.

MRS. PAGE.   On so short an acquaintance?

CHARLES (*lucidly*).   I mean, to have had the priceless cleverness to have her——

MRS. PAGE.   Have her? (*A light breaks on her.*)   My daughter?

CHARLES.   Yes, I know her. (*As who should say, Isn't it a jolly world.*)

MRS. PAGE.   You know Beatrice personally?

CHARLES (*not surprised that it takes her a little time to get used to the idea*).   I assure you I have that honour.   (*In one mouthful*) I think she is the most beautiful and the cleverest woman I have ever known.

MRS. PAGE. I thought I was the cleverest.

CHARLES. Yes, indeed; for I think it even cleverer to have had her than to be her.

MRS. PAGE. Dear me. I must wait till I get a chair before thinking this out. (*A chair means two chairs to her, as we have seen, but she gives the one on which her feet wish to rest to* CHARLES.) You can have this half, Mr.—ah— Mr.—— ?

CHARLES. Roche.

MRS. PAGE (*resting from her labours of the last minute*). You are so flattering, Mr. Roche, I think you must be an actor yourself.

CHARLES (*succinctly*). No, I'm nothing. My father says I'm just an expense. But when I saw Beatrice's photograph there (*the nice boy pauses a moment because this is the first time he has said the name to her mother; he is taking off his hat to it*) with the inscription on it——

MRS. PAGE. That foolish inscription.

CHARLES (*arrested*). Do you think so ?

MRS. PAGE. I mean foolish, because she has

quite spoilt the picture by writing across the chest. That beautiful gown ruined.

CHARLES (*fondly tolerant*). They all do it, even across their trousers ; the men I mean.

MRS. PAGE (*interested*). Do they ? I wonder why.

CHARLES (*remembering now that other callings don't do it*). It does seem odd. (*But after all the others are probably missing something.*)

MRS. PAGE (*shaking her wise head*). I know very little about them, but I am afraid they are an odd race.

CHARLES (*who has doted on many of them, though they were usually not sitting at his table*). But very attractive, don't you think ? The ladies I mean.

MRS. PAGE (*luxuriously*). I mix so little with them. I am not a Bohemian, you see. Did I tell you that I have never even seen Beatrice act ?

CHARLES. You haven't ? How very strange. Not even her Rosalind ?

MRS. PAGE (*stretching herself*). No. Is it cruel to her ?

CHARLES (*giving her one*). Cruel to yourself. (*But this is no policy for an admirer of* MISS PAGE.) She gave me her photograph as Rosalind. (*Hurriedly*) Not a postcard.

MRS. PAGE (*who is very likely sneering*). With writing across the chest, I 'll be bound.

CHARLES (*stoutly*). Do you think I value it the less for that ?

MRS. PAGE (*unblushing*). Oh no, the more. You have it framed on your mantelshelf, haven't you, so that when the other young bloods who are just an expense drop in they may read the pretty words and say, ' Roche, old man, you are going it.'

CHARLES. Do you really think that I——

MRS. PAGE. Pooh, that was what Beatrice expected when she gave it you.

CHARLES. Silence ! (*She raises her eyebrows, and he is stricken.*) I beg your pardon, I should have remembered that you are her mother.

MRS. PAGE (*smiling on him*). I beg yours. I should like to know, Mr. Roche, where you do keep that foolish photograph.

CHARLES (*with a swelling*). Why, here. (*He*

produces it in a case from an honoured pocket.)
Won't you look at it ?

MRS. PAGE (*with proper solemnity*). Yes. It
is one I like.

CHARLES (*cocking his head*). It just misses her
at her best.

MRS. PAGE. Her best ? You mean her way
of screwing her nose ?

CHARLES (*who was never sent up for good for
lucidity—or perhaps he was*). That comes into
it. I mean—I mean her naïveté.

MRS. PAGE. Ah yes, her naïveté. I have
often seen her practising it before a glass.

CHARLES (*with a disarming smile*). Excuse
me ; you haven't, you know.

MRS. PAGE (*disarmed*). Haven't I ? Well,
well, I dare say she is a wonder, but, mind you,
when all is said and done, it is for her nose that
she gets her salary. May I read what is written
on the chest ? (*She reads.*) The baggage !
(*Shaking her head at him*). But this young lady
on the other side, who is she, Lothario ?

CHARLES (*boyish and stumbling*). That is my
sister. She died three years ago. We were

rather—chums—and she gave me that case to put her picture in. So I did.

(*He jerks it out, glaring at her to see if she is despising him. But* MRS. PAGE, *though she cannot be sentimental for long, can be very good at it while it lasts.*)

MRS. PAGE (*quite moved*). Good brother. And it is a dear face. But you should not have put my Beatrice opposite it, Mr. Roche : your sister would not have liked that. It was thoughtless of you.

CHARLES. My sister would have liked it very much. (*Floundering*) When she gave me the case she said to me—you know what girls are— she said, ' If you get to love a woman, put her picture opposite mine, and then when the case is closed I shall be kissing her.'

(*His face implores her not to think him a silly. She is really more troubled than we might have expected.*)

MRS. PAGE (*rising*). Mr. Roche, I never dreamt——

CHARLES. And that is why I keep the two pictures together.

MRS. PAGE. You shouldn't.

CHARLES. Why shouldn't I? Don't you dare to say anything to me against my Beatrice.

MRS. PAGE (*with the smile of ocean on her face*). Your Beatrice. You poor boy.

CHARLES. Of course I haven't any right to call her that. I haven't spoken of it to her yet. I'm such a nobody, you see. (*Very nice and candid of him, but we may remember that his love has not set him trying to make a somebody out of the nobody. Are you perfectly certain,* CHARLES, *that to be seen with the celebrated* PAGE *is not almost more delightful to you than to be with her? Her mother at all events gives him the benefit of the doubt, or so we interpret her sudden action. She tears the photograph in two. He protests indignantly.*)

MRS. PAGE. Mr. Roche, be merry and gay with Beatrice as you will, but don't take her seriously. (*She gives him back the case.*) I think you said you had to catch a train.

CHARLES (*surveying his torn treasure. He is very near to tears, but decides rather recklessly to be a strong man*). Not yet; I must speak of her to you now.

MRS. PAGE (*a strong woman without having to decide*). I forbid you.

CHARLES (*who, if he knew himself, might see that a good deal of gloomy entertainment could be got by desisting here and stalking London as the persecuted of his lady's mamma*). I have the right. There is no decent man who hasn't the right to tell a woman that he loves her daughter.

MRS. PAGE (*determined to keep him to earth though she has to hold him down*). She doesn't love you, my friend.

CHARLES (*though a hopeless passion would be another rather jolly thing*). How do you know ? You have already said——

MRS. PAGE (*rather desperate*). I wish you had never come here.

CHARLES (*manfully*). Why are you so set against me ? I think if I was a woman I should like at any rate to take a good straight look into the eyes of a man who said he was fond of her daughter. You might have to say ' No ' to him, but—often you must have had thoughts of the kind of man who would one day take her from you, and though I may not be the kind, I assure you, I—I am just as fond of her as if I were. (*Not bad for* CHARLES. *Sent up for good this time.*)

MRS. PAGE (*beating her hands together in distress*). You are torturing me, Charles.

CHARLES. But why? Did I tell you my name was Charles? (*With a happy thought*) She has spoken of me to you! What did she say?

> (*If he were thinking less of himself and a little of the woman before him he would see that she has turned into an exquisite supplicant.*)

MRS. PAGE. Oh, boy—you boy! Don't say anything more. Go away now.

CHARLES. I don't understand.

MRS. PAGE. I never had an idea that you cared in that way. I thought we were only jolly friends.

CHARLES. We?

MRS. PAGE (*with a wry lip for the word that has escaped her*). Charles, if you must know, can't you help me out a little? Don't you see at last?

(She has come to him with undulations as lovely as a swallow's flight, mocking, begging, not at all the woman we have been watching; she has become suddenly a disdainful, melting armful. But CHARLES *does not see.)*

CHARLES *(the obtuse)*. I—I——

MRS. PAGE. Very well. But indeed I am sorry to have to break your pretty toy. *(Drooping still farther on her stem.)* Beatrice, Mr. Roche, has not had a mother this many a year. Do you see now?

CHARLES. No.

MRS. PAGE. Well, well. *(Abjectly)* Beatrice, Mr. Roche, is forty and a bittock.

CHARLES. I—you—but—oh no.

MRS. PAGE *(for better, for worse)*. Yes, I am Beatrice. *(He looks to the photograph to rise up and give her the lie.)* The writing on the photograph? A jest. I can explain that.

CHARLES. But—but it isn't only on the stage I have seen her. I know her off too.

MRS. PAGE. A little. I can explain that also. *(He is a very woeful young man.)* I am horribly sorry, Charles.

CHARLES (*with his last kick*).   Even now——

MRS. PAGE.   Do you remember an incident with a pair of scissors one day last June in a boat near Maidenhead ?

CHARLES.   When Beatrice—when you—when she—cut her wrist ?

MRS. PAGE.   And you kissed the place to make it well.   It left its mark.

CHARLES.   I have seen it since.

MRS. PAGE.   You may see it again, Charles. (*She offers him her wrist, but he does not look.   He knows the mark is there.   For the moment the comic spirit has deserted her, so anxious is she to help this tragic boy.   She speaks in the cooing voice that proves her to be* BEATRICE *better than any wrist-mark.*)   Am I so terribly unlike her as you knew her ?

CHARLES (*Ah, to be stabbed with the voice you have loved*).   No. you are very like, only—yes, I know now it's you.

MRS. PAGE (*pricked keenly*).   Only I am looking my age to-day.   (*Forlorn*) This is my real self, Charles—if I have one.   Why don't you laugh, my friend ?   I am laughing.   (*No, not yet,*

though she will be presently.) You won't give me
away, will you ? (*He shakes his head.*) I know
you won't now, but it was my first fear when I
saw you. (*With a sigh*) And now, I suppose, I
owe you an explanation.

CHARLES (*done with the world*). Not unless
you wish to.

MRS. PAGE. Oh yes, I wish to. (*The laughter
is bubbling up now.*) Only it will leave you a
wiser and a sadder man. You will never be
twenty-three again, Charles.

CHARLES (*recalling his distant youth*). No, I
know I won't.

MRS. PAGE (*now the laughter is playing round
her mouth*). Ah, don't take it so lugubriously.
You will only jump to twenty-four, say.
(*She sits down beside him to make full confes-
sion.*) You must often have heard gossip about
actresses' ages ?

CHARLES. I didn't join in it.

MRS. PAGE. Then you can't be a member of
a club.

CHARLES. If they began it——

MRS. PAGE. You wouldn't listen ?

CHARLES. Not about you. I dare say I listened about the others.

MRS. PAGE. You nice boy. And now to make you twenty-four. (*Involuntarily, true to the calling she adorns, she makes the surgeon's action of turning up her sleeves.*) You have seen lots of plays, Charles ?

CHARLES. Yes, tons.

MRS. PAGE. Have you noticed that there are no parts in them for middle-aged ladies ?

CHARLES (*who has had too happy a life to notice this or almost anything else*). Aren't there ?

MRS. PAGE. Oh no, not for ' stars.' There is nothing for them between the ages of twenty-nine and sixty. Occasionally one of the less experienced dramatists may write such a part, but with a little coaxing we can always make him say, ' She needn't be more than twenty-nine.' And so, dear Charles, we have succeeded in keeping middle-age for women off the stage. Why, even Father Time doesn't let on about us. He waits at the wings with a dark cloth for us, just as our dressers wait with dust-sheets to fling over our expensive frocks ; but we have a way with us that makes even Father Time reluctant to cast his cloak; perhaps it is the coquettish imploring look we give him as we dodge him; perhaps though he is an old fellow he can't resist the powder on our pretty noses. And so he says, ' The enchanting baggage, I 'll give her another year.' When you come to write my epitaph, Charles, let it be in these delicious words, ' She had a long twenty-nine.'

CHARLES. But off the stage—I knew you off. (*Recalling a gay phantom*) Why, I was one of those who saw you into your train for Monte Carlo.

MRS. PAGE. You thought you did. That made it easier for me to deceive you here. But I got out of that train at the next station.

> (*She makes a movement to get out of the train here. We begin to note how she suits the action to the word in obedience to Shakespeare's lamentable injunction; she cannot mention the tongs without forking two of her fingers.*)

CHARLES. You came here instead ?

MRS. PAGE. Yes, stole here.

CHARLES (*surveying the broken pieces of her*). Even now I can scarcely— You who seemed so young and gay.

MRS. PAGE (*who is really very good-natured, else would she clout him on the head*). I was a twenty-nine. Oh, don't look so solemn, Charles. It is not confined to the stage. The stalls are full of twenty-nines. Do you remember what fun it was to help me on with my cloak ? Remember why I had to put more powder on my chin one evening ?

CHARLES (*with a groan*). It was only a few weeks ago.

MRS. PAGE. Yes. Sometimes it was Mr. Time I saw in the mirror, but the wretch only winked at me and went his way.

CHARLES (*ungallantly*). But your whole appearance—so girlish compared to——

MRS. PAGE (*gallantly*). To this. I am coming to ' this,' Charles. (*Confidentially ; no one can be quite so delightfully confidential as* BEATRICE PAGE.) You see, never having been more than twenty-nine, not even in my sleep—for we have to keep it up even in our sleep—I began to wonder what middle-age was like. I wanted to feel the sensation. A woman's curiosity, Charles.

CHARLES. Still, you couldn't——

MRS. PAGE. Couldn't I! Listen. Two summers ago, instead of going to Biarritz—see pictures of me in the illustrated papers stepping into my motor-car, or going a round of country houses—see photograph of us all on the steps—the names, Charles, read from left to right—instead of doing any of these things I pretended I went there, and in reality I came down here, determined for a whole calendar month to be a middle-aged lady. I had to get some new clothes, real, cosy, sloppy, very middle-aged clothes ; and that is why I invented mamma ; I got them for her, you see. I said she was about my figure, but stouter and shorter, as you see she is.

CHARLES (*his eyes wandering up and down her—and nowhere a familiar place*). I can't make out——

MRS. PAGE. No, you are too nice a boy to make it out. You don't understand the difference that a sober way of doing one's hair, and

the letting out of a few strings, and sundry
other trifles that are no trifles, make ; but you
see I vowed that if the immortal part of me
was to get a novel sort of rest, my figure should
get it also. *Voilà!* And thus all cosy within
and without, I took lodgings in the most out-of-
the-world spot I knew of, in the hope that here I
might find the lady of whom I was in search.

CHARLES. Meaning ?

MRS. PAGE (*rather grimly*). Meaning myself.
Until two years ago she and I had never met.

CHARLES (*the cynic*). And how do you like her ?

MRS. PAGE. Better than you do, young sir.
She is really rather nice. I don't suppose I
could do with her all the year round, but for
a month or so I am just wallowing in her.
You remember my entrancing little shoes ?
(*she wickedly exposes her flapping slippers*). At
local dances I sit out deliciously as a wall-
flower. Drop a tear, Charles, for me as a wall-
flower. I play cards, and the engaged ladies
give me their confidences as a dear old thing ;
and I never, never dream of setting my cap at
their swains.

CHARLES. How strange. You who, when you liked——

MRS. PAGE (*plaintively*). Yes, couldn't I, Charles?

CHARLES (*falling into the snare*). It was just the wild gaiety of you.

MRS. PAGE (*who is in the better position to know*). It was the devilry of me.

CHARLES. Whatever it was, it bewitched us.

MRS. PAGE (*candidly, but forgiving herself*). It oughtn't to.

CHARLES. If you weren't all glee you were the saddest thing on earth.

MRS. PAGE. But I shouldn't have been sad on your shoulders, Charles.

CHARLES (*appealing*). You weren't sad on all our shoulders, were you?

MRS. PAGE (*reassuring*). No, not all.

> Oh the gladness of her gladness when she's glad,
> And the sadness of her sadness when she's sad,
> But the gladness of her gladness
> And the sadness of her sadness
> Are as nothing, Charles,
> To the badness of her badness when she's bad.

(*This dagger-to-her-breast business is one*

H

of her choicest tricks of fence, and is very
dangerous if you can coo like BEATRICE.)

CHARLES (*pinked*). Not a word against yourself.

MRS. PAGE (*already seeing what she has been*
up to). Myself! I suppose even now I am
only playing a part.

CHARLES (*who has become her handkerchief*).
No, no, this is your real self.

MRS. PAGE (*warily*). Is it? I wonder.

CHARLES. I never knew any one who had
deeper feelings.

MRS. PAGE. Oh, I am always ready with
whatever feeling is called for. I have a ward-
robe of them, Charles. Don't blame me, blame
the public of whom you are one; the pitiless
public that has made me what I am. I am
their slave and their plaything, and when I
please them they fling me nuts. (*Her voice*
breaks; no voice can break so naturally as
BEATRICE'S.) I would have been a darling of
a wife—don't you think so, Charles?—but they
wouldn't let me. I am only a bundle of
emotions; I have two characters for each day
of the week. Home became a less thing to me

than a new part. Charles, if only I could have
been a nobody. Can't you picture me, such
a happy, unknown woman, dancing along some
sandy shore with half a dozen little boys and
girls hanging on to my skirts? When my son
was old enough, wouldn't he and I have made a
rather pretty picture for the king the day he
joined his ship. And I think most of all I
should have loved to deck out my daughter
in her wedding-gown.

> When her mother tends her before the laughing
> mirror,
> Tying up her laces, looping up her hair—

But the public wouldn't have it, and I had to
pay the price of my success.

CHARLES (*heart-broken for that wet face*).
Beatrice !

MRS. PAGE. I became a harum-scarum,
Charles; sometimes very foolish—(*with a queer
insight into herself*) chiefly through good-nature,
I think. There were moments when there was
nothing I wouldn't do, so long as I was all right
for the play at night. Nothing else seemed to

matter. I have kicked over all the traces, my friend. You remember the Scottish poet who

> Keenly felt the friendly glow
> And softer flame,
> But thoughtless follies laid him low
> And stained his name.

(*Sadly enough*) Thoughtless follies laid her low, Charles, and stained her name.

CHARLES (*ready to fling down his glove in her defence*). I don't believe it. No, no, Beatrice —Mrs. Page——

MRS. PAGE. Ah, it's Mrs. Page now.

CHARLES. You are crying.

MRS. PAGE (*with some satisfaction*). Yes, I am crying.

CHARLES. This is terrible to me. I never dreamt your life was such a tragedy.

MRS. PAGE (*coming to*). Don't be so concerned. I am crying, but all the time I am looking at you through the corner of my eye to see if I am doing it well.

CHARLES (*hurt*). Don't—don't.

MRS. PAGE (*well aware that she will always be her best audience*). Soon I'll be laughing again.

When I have cried, Charles, then it is time for me to laugh.

CHARLES. Please, I wish you wouldn't.

MRS. PAGE (*already in the grip of another devil*). And from all this, Charles, you have so nobly offered to save me. You are prepared to take me away from this dreadful life and let me be my real self. (CHARLES *distinctly blanches*.) Charles, it is dear and kind of you, and I accept your offer. (*She gives him a come-and-take-me curtsy and awaits his rapturous response. The referee counts ten, but* CHARLES *has not risen from the floor. Goose that he is; she trills with merriment, though there is a touch of bitterness in it.*) You see the time for laughing has come already. You really thought I wanted you, you conceited boy. (*Rather grandly*) I am not for the likes of you.

CHARLES (*abject*). Don't mock me. I am very unhappy.

MRS. PAGE (*putting her hand on his shoulder in her dangerous, careless, kindly way*). There, there, it is just a game. All life's a game.

(*It is here that the telegram comes.* MRS.

QUICKLY *brings it in; and the better to read it, but with a glance at* CHARLES *to observe the effect on him,* MRS. PAGE *puts on her large horn spectacles. He sighs.*)

DAME. Is there any answer? The girl is waiting.

MRS. PAGE. No answer, thank you.

(MRS. QUICKLY *goes, wondering what those two have had to say to each other.*)

CHARLES (*glad to be a thousand miles away from recent matters*). Not bad news, I hope?

MRS. PAGE (*wiping her spectacles*). From my manager. It is in cipher, but what it means is that the summer play isn't drawing, and that they have decided to revive *As You Like It.* They want me back to rehearse to-morrow at eleven.

CHARLES (*indignant*). They can't even let you have a few weeks.

MRS. PAGE (*returning from London*). What? Heigho, is it not sad? But I had been warned that this might happen.

CHARLES (*evolving schemes*). Surely if you——

(*But she has summoned* MRS. QUICKLY.)

MRS. PAGE (*plaintively*). Alas, Dame, our pleasant gossips have ended for this year. I am called back to London hurriedly.

DAME. Oh dear, the pity ! (*She has already asked herself what might be in the telegram.*) Your girl has come back, and she wants you ? Is that it ?

MRS. PAGE. That's about it. (*Her quiet, sad manner says that we must all dree our weird.*) I must go. Have I time to catch the express ?

CHARLES (*dispirited*). It leaves at seven.

MRS. PAGE (*bravely*). I think I can do it. Is that the train you are to take ?

CHARLES. Yes, but only to the next station.

MRS. PAGE (*grown humble in her misfortune*). Even for that moment of your company I shall be grateful. Dame, this gentleman turns out to be a friend of Beatrice.

DAME. So he said, but I suspicioned him.

MRS. PAGE. Well, he is. Mr. Roche, this is my kind Dame. I must put a few things together.

DAME. If I can help——

MRS. PAGE. You can send on my luggage to-morrow; but here is one thing you might do now. Run down to the Rectory and tell them why I can't be there for the cutting-out.

DAME. I will.

MRS. PAGE. I haven't many minutes. Good-bye, you dear, for I shall be gone before you get back. I'll write and settle everything. (*With a last look round*) Cosy room! I have had a lovely time.

> (*Her face quivers a little, but she does not break down. She passes, a courageous figure, into the bedroom. The slippers plop as she mounts the steps to it. Her back looks older than we have seen it; at least such is its intention.*)

DAME (*who has learned the uselessness of railing against fate*). Dearie dear, what a pity.

CHARLES (*less experienced*). It's horrible.

DAME (*wisely turning fate into a gossip*). Queer to think of a lady like Mrs. Page having a daughter that jumps about for a living. (*Good God, thinks* CHARLES, *how little this woman knows of life.*) What I sometimes fear is that the daughter doesn't take much care of her. I dare say she 's fond of her, but does she do the little kind things for her that a lady come Mrs. Page's age needs ?

CHARLES (*wincing*).   She 's not so old.

DAME (*whose mind is probably running on breakfast in bed and such-like matters*).   No, but at our age we are fond of—of quiet, and I doubt she doesn't get it.

CHARLES.   I know she doesn't.

DAME (*stumbling among fine words which attract her like a display of drapery*).   She says it 's her right to be out of the hurly-burly and into what she calls the delicious twilight of middle-age.

CHARLES (*with dizzying thoughts in his brain*). If she is so fond of it, isn't it a shame she should have to give it up ?

DAME.   The living here ?

CHARLES.   Not so much that as being middle-aged.

DAME.   Give up being middle-aged !   How could she do that ?

(*He is saved replying by* MRS. PAGE, *who calls from the bedroom.*)

MRS. PAGE. Dame, I hear you talking, and you promised to go at once.

> (*The* DAME *apologises, and is off.* CHARLES *is left alone with his great resolve, which is no less than to do one of the fine things of history. It carries him toward the bedroom door, but not quickly ; one can also see that it has a rival who is urging him to fly the house.*)

CHARLES (*with a drum beating inside him*). Beatrice, I want to speak to you at once.

MRS. PAGE (*through the closed door*). As soon as I have packed my bag.

CHARLES (*finely*). Don't pack it.

MRS. PAGE. I must.

CHARLES. I have something to say.

MRS. PAGE. I can hear you.

CHARLES (*who had been honourably mentioned for the school prize poem*). Beatrice, until now I hadn't really known you at all. The girl I was so fond of, there wasn't any such girl.

MRS. PAGE. Oh yes, indeed there was.

CHARLES (*now in full sail for a hero's crown*). There was the dear woman who was Rosalind,

but she had tired of it. Rosalind herself grew
old and gave up the forest of Arden, but there
was one man who never forgot the magic of her
being there; and I shall never forget yours.
(*Strange that between the beatings of the drum he
should hear a little voice within him calling, ' Ass,
Charles, you ass ! ' or words to that effect. But
he runs nobly on.*) My dear, I want to be your
Orlando to the end. (*Surely nothing could be
grander. He is chagrined to get no response
beyond what might be the breaking of a string.*)
Do you hear me ?

MRS. PAGE. Yes. (*A brief answer, but he is
off again.*)

CHARLES. I will take you out of that hurly-
burly and accompany you into the delicious
twilight of middle-age. I shall be staid in
manner so as not to look too young, and I will
make life easy for you in your declining years.
('*Ass, Charles, you ass !*') Beatrice, do come out.

MRS. PAGE. I am coming now. (*She cómes
out carrying her bag.*) You naughty Charles, I
heard you proposing to mamma.

(*The change that has come over her is far*

*too subtle to have grown out of a wish to
surprise him, but its effect on* CHARLES *is
as if she had struck him in the face.*

*Too subtle also to be only an affair of
clothes, though she is now in bravery hot
from Mdme. Make-the-woman, tackle by
Monsieur, a Rosalind cap jaunty on her
head, her shoes so small that one wonders if
she ever has to light a candle to look for her
feet. She is a tall, slim young creature,
easily breakable;* svelte *is the word that
encompasses her as we watch the flow of
her figure, her head arching on its long
stem, and the erect shoulders that we seem,
God bless us, to remember as a little hunched.
Her eyes dance with life but are easily
startled, because they are looking fresh
upon the world, wild notes in them as from
the woods. Not a woman this but a maid,
or so it seems to* CHARLES.

*She has been thinking very little about
him, but is properly gratified by what she
reads in his face.*)

Do I surprise you as much as that, Charles?

(She puts down her bag, BEATRICE PAGE'S *famous bag. If you do not know it, you do not, alas, know* BEATRICE. *It is seldom out of her hand, save when cavaliers have been sent in search of it. She is always late for everything except her call, and at the last moment she sweeps all that is most precious to her into the bag, and runs. Jewels? Oh no, pooh; letters from no-bodies, postal orders for them, a piece of cretonne that must match she forgets what, bits of string she forgets why, a book given her by darling What's-his-name, a broken miniature, part of a watch-chain, a dog's collar, such a neat parcel tied with ribbon (golden gift or biscuits? she means to find out some day), a purse, but not the right one, a bottle of frozen gum, and a hundred good-natured, scatter-brained things besides. Her servants (who all adore her) hate the bag as if it were a little dog; swains hate it because it gets lost and has to be found in the middle of a declaration; managers hate it because she*

carries it at rehearsals, when it bursts open suddenly like a too tightly laced lady, and its contents are strewn on the stage; authors make engaging remarks about it until they discover that it has an artful trick of bursting because she does not know her lines. If you complain, really furious this time, she takes you all in her arms. Well, well, but what we meant to say was that when BEATRICE *sees* CHARLES'S *surprise she puts down her bag.*)

CHARLES.   Good God ! Is there nothing real in life ?

(*She curves toward him in one of those swallow-flights which will haunt the stage long after* BEATRICE PAGE *is but a memory. What they say and how they said it soon passes away; what lives on is the pretty movements like* BEATRICE'S *swallow-flights. All else may go, but the pretty movements remain and play about the stage for ever. They are the only ghosts of the theatre.*)

MRS. PAGE. Heaps of things. Rosalind is real, and I am Rosalind; and the forest of

Arden is real, and I am going back to it; and
cakes and ale are real, and I am to eat and
drink them again. Everything is real except
middle-age.

> (*She puts her hand on his shoulder in the
> old, dangerous, kindly, too friendly way.
> That impulsive trick of yours, madam,
> has a deal to answer for.*)

CHARLES. But you said——

> (*She flings up her hands in mockery;
> they are such subtle hands that she can
> stand with her back to you, and, put-
> ting them behind her, let them play the
> drama.*)

MRS. PAGE. I said! (*She is gone from him
in another flight.*) I am Rosalind and I am
going back. Hold me down, Charles, unless
you want me to go mad with glee.

CHARLES (*gripping her*). I feel as if in the
room you came out of you have left the woman
who went into it five minutes ago.

MRS. PAGE (*slipping from him as she slips from
all of us*). I have, Charles, I have. I left the
floppy, sloppy old frump in a trunk to be carted

to the nearest place where they store furniture ; and I tell you, my friend (*she might have said friends, for it is a warning to the Charleses of every age*), if I had a husband and children I would cram them on top of the cart if they sought to come between me and Arden.

CHARLES (*with a shiver*). Beatrice !

MRS. PAGE. The stage is waiting, the audience is calling, and up goes the curtain. Oh, my public, my little dears, come and foot it again in the forest, and tuck away your double chins.

CHARLES. You said you hated the public.

MRS. PAGE. It was mamma said that. They are my slaves and my playthings, and I toss them nuts. (*He knows not how she got there, but for a moment of time her head caressingly skims his shoulder, and she is pouting in his face.*) Every one forgives me but you, Charles, every one but you.

CHARLES (*delirious*). Beatrice, you unutterable delight——

MRS. PAGE (*worlds away*). Don't forgive me if you would rather not,

> Here 's a sigh to those who love me,
> And a smile to those who hate.

CHARLES (*pursuing her*). There is no one like you on earth, Beatrice. Marry me, marry me (*as if he could catch her*).

MRS. PAGE (*cruelly*). As a staff for my declining years ?

CHARLES. Forget that rubbish and marry me, you darling girl.

MRS. PAGE. I can't and I won't, but I 'm glad I am your darling girl. (*Very likely she is about to be delightful to him, but suddenly she sees her spoil-sport of a bag.*) I am trusting to you not to let me miss the train.

CHARLES. I am coming with you all the way (*as if she needed to be told*). We had better be off.

MRS. PAGE (*seizing the bag*). Charles, as we run to the station we will stop at every telegraph post and carve something sweet on it—' From the East to Western Ind '——

CHARLES (*inspired*). ' No jewel is like Rosalind '——

MRS. PAGE. ' Middle-age is left behind '——

I

CHARLES. 'For ever young is Rosalind.'
Oh, you dear, Motley's the only wear.

MRS. PAGE. And all the way up in the train,
Charles, you shall woo me exquisitely. Nothing
will come of it, but you are twenty-three again,
and you will have a lovely time.

CHARLES. I'll win you, I'll win you.

MRS. PAGE. And eventually you will marry
the buxom daughter of the wealthy tallow-
chandler——

CHARLES. Never, I swear.

MRS. PAGE (*screwing her nose*). And bring
your children to see me playing the Queen in
Hamlet.

(*Here* CHARLES ROCHE, *bachelor, kisses
the famous* BEATRICE PAGE. *Another
sound is heard.*)

CHARLES. The whistle of the train.

MRS. PAGE. Away, away! 'Tis Touchstone
calling. Fool, I come, I come. (*To bedroom
door*) Ta-ta, mamma.

(*They are gone.*)

THE WILL

THE WILL

The scene is any lawyer's office.

*It may be, and no doubt will be, the minute repro-
duction of some actual office, with all the characteristic
appurtenances thereof, every blot of ink in its proper
place ; but for the purpose in hand any bare room
would do just as well. The only thing essential to
the room, save the two men sitting in it, is a framed
engraving on the wall of Queen Victoria, which dates
sufficiently the opening scene, and will be changed
presently to King Edward ; afterwards to King
George, to indicate the passing of time. No other
alteration is called for. Doubtless different furniture
came in, and the tiling of the fireplace was renewed,
and at last some one discovered that the flowers in the
window-box were dead, but all that is as immaterial
to the action as the new blue-bottles ; the succession of
monarchs will convey allegorically the one thing
necessary, that time is passing, but that the office of
Devizes, Devizes, and Devizes goes on.*

The two men are Devizes Senior and Junior.

Senior, who is middle-aged, succeeded to a good thing years ago, and as the curtain rises we see him bent over his table making it a better thing. It is pleasant to think that before he speaks he adds another thirteen and fourpence, say, to the fortune of the firm.

Junior is quite a gay dog, twenty-three, and we catch him skilfully balancing an office ruler on his nose. He is recently from Oxford—

If you show him in Hyde Park, lawk, how they will
    stare,
Tho' a very smart figure in Bloomsbury Square.

Perhaps Junior is a smarter figure in the office (among the clerks) than he was at Oxford, but this is one of the few things about him that his shrewd father does not know.

There comes to them by the only door into the room a middle-aged clerk called Surtees, who is perhaps worth looking at, though his manner is that of one who has long ceased to think of himself as of any import-ance to either God or man. Look at him again, however (which few would do), and you may guess that he has lately had a shock—touched a living wire— and is a little dazed by it. He brings a card to Mr. Devizes, Senior, who looks at it and shakes his head.

MR. DEVIZES. 'Mr. Philip Ross.' Don't know him.

SURTEES (*who has an expressionless voice*). He says he wrote you two days ago, sir, explaining his business.

MR. DEVIZES. I have had no letter from a Philip Ross.

ROBERT. Nor I.

(*He is more interested in his feat with the ruler than in a possible client, but* SURTEES *looks at him oddly.*)

MR. DEVIZES. Surtees looks as if he thought you had.

(ROBERT *obliges by reflecting in the light of* SURTEES'S *countenance.*)

ROBERT. Ah, you think it may have been that one, Surty ?

MR. DEVIZES (*sharply*). What one ?

ROBERT. It was the day before yesterday. You were out, father, and Surtees brought me in some letters. His mouth was wide open. (*Thoughtfully*) I suppose that was why I did it.

MR. DEVIZES. What did you do ?

ROBERT. I must have suddenly recalled a

game we used to play at Oxford. You try to fling cards one by one into a hat. It requires great skill. So I cast one of the letters at Surtees's open mouth, and it missed him and went into the fire. It may have been Philip Ross's letter.

MR. DEVIZES (*wrinkling his brows*). Too bad, Robert.

ROBERT (*blandly*). Yes, you see I am out of practice.

SURTEES. He seemed a very nervous person, sir, and quite young. Not a gentleman of much consequence.

ROBERT (*airily*). Why not tell him to write again ?

MR. DEVIZES. Not fair.

SURTEES. But she——

ROBERT. She ? Who ?

SURTEES. There is a young lady with him, sir. She is crying.

ROBERT. Pretty ?

SURTEES. I should say she is pretty, sir, in a quite inoffensive way.

ROBERT (*for his own gratification*). Ha !

MR. DEVIZES. Well, when I ring show them in.

ROBERT (*with roguish finger*). And let this be a lesson to you, Surty, not to go about your business with your mouth open. (SURTEES *tries to smile as requested, but with poor success.*) Nothing the matter, Surty? You seem to have lost your sense of humour.

SURTEES (*humbly enough*). I'm afraid I have, sir. I never had very much, Mr. Robert.

> (*He goes quietly. There has been a suppressed emotion about him that makes the incident poignant.*)

ROBERT. Anything wrong with Surtees, father?

MR. DEVIZES. Never mind him. I am very angry with you, Robert.

ROBERT (*like one conceding a point in a debating society*). And justly.

MR. DEVIZES (*frowning*). All we can do is to tell this Mr. Ross that we have not read his letter.

ROBERT (*bringing his knowledge of the world to bear*). Is that necessary?

MR. DEVIZES. We must admit that we don't know what he has come about.

ROBERT (*tolerant of his father's limitations*). But don't we ?

MR. DEVIZES. Do you ?

ROBERT. I rather think I can put two and two together.

MR. DEVIZES. Clever boy ! Well, I shall leave them to you.

ROBERT. Right.

MR. DEVIZES. Your first case, Robert.

ROBERT (*undismayed*). It will be as good as a play to you to sit there and watch me discovering before they have been two minutes in the room what is the naughty thing that brings them here.

MR. DEVIZES (*drily*). I am always ready to take a lesson from the new generation. But of course we old fogies could do that also.

ROBERT. How ?

MR. DEVIZES. By asking them.

ROBERT. Pooh. What did I go to Oxford for ?

MR. DEVIZES. God knows. Are you ready ?

ROBERT. Quite.

(MR. DEVIZES *rings*.)

MR. DEVIZES. By the way, we don't know
the lady's name.

ROBERT. Observe me finding it out.

MR. DEVIZES. Is she married or single ?

ROBERT. I'll know at a glance. And mark
me, if she is married it is our nervous gentleman
who has come between her and her husband ;
but if she is single it is little Wet Face who has
come between him and his wife.

MR. DEVIZES. A Daniel !

> (*A young man and woman are shown in :
> very devoted to each other, though* ROBERT
> *does not know it. Yet it is the one thing
> obvious about them ; more obvious than
> his cheap suit, which she presses carefully
> beneath the mattress every night, or than
> the strength of his boyish face. Thinking
> of him as he then was by the light of sub-
> sequent events one wonders whether if he
> had come alone his face might have revealed
> something disquieting which was not there
> while she was by. Probably not ; it was
> certainly already there, but had not yet
> reached the surface. With her, too, though*

*she is to be what is called changed before
we see them again, all seems serene; no
warning signals; nothing in the way of
their happiness in each other but this
alarming visit to a lawyer's office. The
stage direction might be ' Enter two lovers.'
He is scarcely the less nervous of the
two, but he enters stoutly in front of her
as if to receive the first charge. She
has probably nodded valiantly to him
outside the door, where she let go his
hand.)*

ROBERT (*master of the situation*). Come in,
Mr. Ross (*and he bows reassuringly to the lady*).
My partner—indeed my father. (MR. DEVIZES
bows but remains in the background.)

PHILIP (*with a gulp*). You got my letter?

ROBERT. Yes—yes.

PHILIP. I gave you the details in it.

ROBERT. Yes, I have them all in my head.
(*Cleverly*) You will sit down Miss— I don't
think I caught the name.

(*As much as to say, ' You see, father, I
spotted that she was single at once.'*)

MR. DEVIZES (*who has also formed his opinion*). You didn't ask for it, Robert.

ROBERT (*airily*). Miss—— ?

PHILIP.   This is Mrs. Ross, my wife.

> (ROBERT *is a little taken aback, and has a conviction that his father is smiling.*)

ROBERT.   Ah yes, of course ;   sit down, please, Mrs. Ross.

> (*She sits as if this made matters rather worse.*)

PHILIP (*standing guard by her side*).   My wife is a little agitated.

ROBERT.   Naturally. (*He tries a ' feeler.'*) These affairs—very painful at the time—but one gradually forgets.

EMILY (*with large eyes*).   That is what Mr. Ross says, but somehow I can't help — (*the eyes fill*).   You see, we have been married only four months.

ROBERT.   Ah—that does make it—yes, certainly. (*He becomes the wife's champion, and frowns on* PHILIP.)

PHILIP.   I suppose the sum seems very small to you ?

ROBERT (*serenely*). I confess that is the impression it makes on me.

PHILIP. I wish it was more.

ROBERT (*at a venture*). You are sure you can't make it more ?

PHILIP. How can I ?

ROBERT. Ha !

EMILY (*with sudden spirit*). I think it's a great deal.

PHILIP. Mrs. Ross is so nice about it.

ROBERT (*taking a strong line*). I think so. But she must not be taken advantage of. And of course we shall have something to say as to the amount.

PHILIP (*blankly*). In what way ? There it is.

ROBERT (*guardedly*). Hum. Yes, in a sense.

EMILY (*breaking down*). Oh dear !

ROBERT (*more determined than ever to do his best for this wronged woman*). I am very sorry, Mrs. Ross. (*Sternly*) I hope, sir, you realise that the mere publicity to a sensitive woman——

PHILIP. Publicity ?

ROBERT (*feeling that he has got him on the run*). Of course for her sake we shall try to

arrange things so that the names do not appear.
Still——

PHILIP. The names ?

(*By this time* EMILY *is in tears.*)

EMILY. I can't help it. I love him so.

ROBERT (*still benighted*). Enough to forgive
him ? (*Seeing himself suddenly as a mediator*)
Mrs. Ross, is it too late to patch things up ?

PHILIP (*now in flame*). What do you mean,
sir ?

MR. DEVIZES (*who has been quietly enjoying
himself*). Yes, Robert, what do you mean
precisely ?

ROBERT. Really I—(*he tries brow-beating*)
I must tell you at once, Mr. Ross, that unless a
client gives us his fullest confidence we cannot
undertake a case of this kind.

PHILIP. A case of what kind, sir ? If you
are implying anything against my good name——

ROBERT. On your honour, sir, is there nothing
against it ?

PHILIP. I know of nothing, sir.

EMILY. Anything against my husband, Mr.
Devizes ! He is an angel.

ROBERT (*suddenly seeing that little Wet Face must be the culprit*). Then it is you !

EMILY. Oh, sir, what is me ?

PHILIP. Answer that, sir.

ROBERT. Yes, Mr. Ross, I will. (*But he finds he cannot.*) On second thoughts I decline. I cannot believe it has been all this lady's fault, and I decline to have anything to do with such a painful case.

MR. DEVIZES (*promptly*). Then I will take it up.

PHILIP (*not to be placated*). I think your son has insulted me.

EMILY. Philip, come away.

MR. DEVIZES. One moment, please. As *I* did not see your letter, may I ask Mr. Ross what is your business with us ?

PHILIP. I called to ask whether you would be so good as to draw up my will.

ROBERT (*blankly*). Your will ! Is that all ?

PHILIP. Certainly.

MR. DEVIZES. Now we know, Robert.

ROBERT. But Mrs. Ross's agitation ?

PHILIP (*taking her hand*). She feels that to make my will brings my death nearer.

ROBERT. So that's it!

PHILIP. It was all in the letter.

MR. DEVIZES (*coyly*). Anything to say, Robert?

ROBERT. Most—ah—extremely— (*He has an inspiration.*) But even now I'm puzzled. You are Edgar Charles Ross?

PHILIP. No, Philip Ross.

ROBERT (*brazenly*). Philip Ross? We have made an odd mistake, father. (*There is a twinkle in* MR. DEVIZES'S *eye. He watches interestedly to see how his son is to emerge from the mess.*) The fact is, Mrs. Ross, we are expecting to-day a Mr. Edgar Charles Ross on a matter—well—of a kind— Ah me. (*With fitting gravity*) His wife, in short.

EMILY (*who has not read the newspapers in vain*). How awful. How sad.

ROBERT. Sad indeed. You will quite understand that professional etiquette prevents my saying one word more.

PHILIP. Yes, of course—we have no desire— But I did write.

ROBERT. Assuredly. But about a will.

K

That is my father's department. No doubt
you recall the letter now, father ?

MR. DEVIZES (*who if he won't hinder won't help*).
I can't say I do.

ROBERT (*unabashed*). Odd. You must have
overlooked it.

MR. DEVIZES. Ha. At all events, Mr. Ross,
I am quite at your service now.

PHILIP. Thank you.

ROBERT (*still ready to sacrifice himself on the
call of duty*). You don't need me any more,
father ?

MR. DEVIZES. No, Robert ; many thanks.
You run off to your club now and have a bit of
lunch. You must be tired. Send Surtees in to
me. (*To his clients*) My son had his first case
to-day.

PHILIP (*politely*). I hope successfully.

MR. DEVIZES. Not so bad. He rather bungled
it at first, but he got out of a hole rather cleverly.
I think you 'll make a lawyer yet, Robert.

ROBERT. Thank you, father. (*He goes
jauntily, with a flower in his button-hole.*)

MR. DEVIZES. Now, Mr. Ross.

(The young wife's hand goes out for comfort and finds PHILIP'S *waiting for it.)*

PHILIP. What I want myself is that the will should all go into one sentence, 'I leave everything of which I die possessed to my beloved wife.'

MR. DEVIZES (*thawing to the romance of this young couple*). Well, there have been many worse wills than that, sir.

(EMILY *is emotional.*)

PHILIP. Don't give way, Emily.

EMILY. It was those words, 'of which I die possessed.' (*Imploring*) Surely he doesn't need to say that—please, Mr. Devizes?

MR. DEVIZES. Certainly not. I am confident I can draw up the will without mentioning death at all.

EMILY (*huskily*). Oh, thank you.

MR. DEVIZES. At the same time, of course, in a legal document in which the widow is the sole——

(EMILY *again needs attention.*)

PHILIP (*reproachfully*). What was the need of saying ' widow ' ?

MR. DEVIZES. I beg your pardon, Mrs. Ross. I unreservedly withdraw the word ' widow.' Forgive a stupid old solicitor. (*She smiles gratefully through her tears.* SURTEES *comes in.*) Surtees, just take a few notes, please. (SURTEES *sits in the background and takes notes.*) The facts of the case as I understand, Mrs. Ross, are these : Your husband—(*Quickly*) who is in the prime of health—but knows life to be uncertain——

EMILY. Oh !

MR. DEVIZES. —though usually, as we learn from holy script itself, it lasts seven times ten years—and believing that he will in all probability live the allotted span, nevertheless, because of his love of you, thinks it judicious to go through the form—it is a mere form—of making a will.

EMILY (*fervently*). Oh, thank you.

MR. DEVIZES. Any details, Mr. Ross ?

PHILIP. I am an orphan. I live at Belvedere, 14 Tulphin Road, Hammersmith.

EMILY (*to whom the address has a seductive sound*). We live there.

PHILIP. And I am a clerk in the employ of Curar and Gow, the foreign coaling agents.

MR. DEVIZES. Yes, yes. Any private income?

(*They cannot help sniggering a little at the quaint question.*)

PHILIP. Oh no!

MR. DEVIZES. I see it will be quite a brief will.

PHILIP (*to whom the remark sounds scarcely worthy of a great occasion*). My income is a biggish one.

MR. DEVIZES. Yes?

EMILY (*important*). He has £170 a year.

MR. DEVIZES. Ah.

PHILIP. I began at £60. But it is going up, Mr. Devizes, by leaps and bounds. Another £15 this year.

MR. DEVIZES. Good.

PHILIP (*darkly*). I have a certain ambition.

EMILY (*eagerly*). Tell him, Philip.

PHILIP (*with a big breath*). We have made up our minds to come to £365 a year before I —retire.

EMILY. That is a pound a day.

MR. DEVIZES (*smiling sympathetically on them*). So it is. My best wishes.

PHILIP. Thank you. Of course the furnishing took a good deal.

MR. DEVIZES. It would.

EMILY. He insisted on my having the very best. (*She ceases. She is probably thinking of her superb spare bedroom.*)

PHILIP. But we are not a penny in debt; and I have £200 saved.

MR. DEVIZES. I think you have made a brave beginning.

EMILY. They have the highest opinion of him in the office.

PHILIP. Then I am insured for £500.

MR. DEVIZES. I am glad to hear that.

PHILIP. Of course I would like to leave her a house in Kensington and a carriage and pair.

MR. DEVIZES. Who knows, perhaps you will.

EMILY. Oh !

MR. DEVIZES. Forgive me.

EMILY. What would houses and horses be to me without him ?

MR. DEVIZES (*soothingly*). Quite so. What I take Mr. Ross to mean is that when he dies—if he ever should die—everything is to go to his—his spouse.

PHILIP (*dogged*). Yes.

EMILY (*dogged*). No.

PHILIP (*sighing*). This is the only difference we have ever had. Mrs. Ross insists on certain bequests. You see, I have two cousins, ladies, not well off, whom I have been in the way of helping a little. But in my will, how can I ?

MR. DEVIZES. You must think first of your wife.

PHILIP. But she insists on my leaving £50 to each of them.

(*He looks appealingly to his wife.*)

EMILY (*grandly*). £100.

PHILIP. £50.

EMILY. Dear, £100.

MR. DEVIZES. Let us say £75.

PHILIP (*reluctantly*). Very well.

EMILY. No, £100.

PHILIP. She 'll have to get her way. Here are their names and addresses.

MR. DEVIZES. Anything else ?

PHILIP (*hurriedly*). No.

EMILY. The convalescent home, dear. He was in it a year ago, and they were so kind.

PHILIP. Yes, but——

EMILY. £10. (*He has to yield, with a reproachful, admiring look.*)

MR. DEVIZES. Then if that is all, I won't detain you. If you look in to-morrow, Mr. Ross, about this time, we shall have everything ready for you.

(*Their faces fall.*)

EMILY. Oh, Mr. Devizes, if only it could all be drawn up now, and done with.

PHILIP. You see, sir, we are screwed up to it to-day.

> (' *Our fate is in your hands,*' they might
> be saying, and the lawyer smiles to find
> himself such a power.)

MR. DEVIZES (*looking at his watch*). Well, it certainly need not take long. You go out and have lunch somewhere, and then come back.

EMILY. Oh, don't ask me to eat.

PHILIP. We are too excited.

EMILY.   Please may we just walk about the
street ?

MR. DEVIZES (*smiling*).   Of course you may,
you ridiculous young wife.

EMILY.   I know it 's ridiculous of me, but
I am so fond of him.

MR. DEVIZES.   Yes, it is ridiculous. (*Kindly,
and with almost a warning note*) But don't
change ; especially if you get on in the world,
Mr. Ross.

PHILIP.   No fear !

EMILY (*backing from the will, which may now
be said to be in existence*).   And please don't
give us a copy of it to keep.   I would rather
not have it in the house.

MR. DEVIZES (*nodding reassuringly*).   In an
hour's time.   (*They go, and the lawyer has his
lunch, which is simpler than* ROBERT'S : *a sand-
wich and a glass of wine.   He speaks as he eats.*)
You will get that ready, Surtees.   Here are
the names and addresses he left.   (*Cheerily*) A
nice couple.

SURTEES (*who is hearing another voice*).   Yes,
sir.

MR. DEVIZES (*unbending*). Little romance of its kind. Makes one feel quite gay.

SURTEES. Yes, sir.

MR. DEVIZES (*struck perhaps by the deadness of his voice*). You don't look very gay, Surtees.

SURTEES. I'm sorry, sir. We can't all be gay. (*He is going out without looking at his employer.*) I'll see to this, sir.

MR. DEVIZES. Stop a minute. Is there anything wrong? (SURTEES *has difficulty in answering, and* MR. DEVIZES *goes to him kindly.*) Not worrying over that matter we spoke about? (SURTEES *inclines his head.*) Is the pain worse?

SURTEES. It's no great pain, sir.

MR. DEVIZES (*uncomfortably*). I'm sure it's not—what you fear. Any specialist would tell you so.

SURTEES (*without looking up*). I have been to one, sir—yesterday.

MR. DEVIZES. Well?

SURTEES. It's—that, sir.

MR. DEVIZES. He couldn't be sure.

SURTEES. Yes, sir.

MR. DEVIZES. An operation——

SURTEES. Too late, he said, for that. If I had been operated on long ago there might have been a chance.

MR. DEVIZES. But you didn't have it long ago.

SURTEES. Not to my knowledge, sir; but he says it was there all the same, always in me, a black spot, not so big as a pin's head, but waiting to spread and destroy me in the fulness of time. All the rest of me as sound as a bell. (*That is the voice that* SURTEES *has been hearing*.)

MR. DEVIZES (*helpless*). It seems damnably unfair.

SURTEES (*humbly*). I don't know, sir. He says there's a spot of that kind in pretty nigh all of us, and if we don't look out it does for us in the end.

MR. DEVIZES (*hurriedly*). No, no, no.

SURTEES. He called it the accursed thing. I think he meant we should know of it and be on the watch. (*He pulls himself together*.) I'll see to this at once, sir.

> (*He goes out.* MR. DEVIZES *continues his lunch.*

The curtain falls here for a moment only, to indicate the passing of a number of years. When it rises we see that the engraving of Queen Victoria has given way to one of King Edward.

ROBERT *is discovered, immersed in affairs. He is now a middle-aged man who has long forgotten how to fling cards into a hat. To him comes* SENNET, *a brisk clerk.*)

SENNET.   Mrs. Philip Ross to see you, sir.

ROBERT.   Mr. Ross, don't you mean, Sennet ?

SENNET.   No, sir.

ROBERT.   Ha. It was Mr. Ross I was expecting. Show her in. (*Frowning*) And, Sennet, less row in the office, if you please.

SENNET (*glibly*).   It was those young clerks, sir——

ROBERT.   They mustn't be young here, or they go. Tell them that.

SENNET (*glad to be gone*).   Yes, sir.

(*He shows in* MRS. ROSS. *We have not seen her for twenty years and would certainly not recognise her in the street. So shrinking*

*her first entrance into this room, but she
sails in now like a galleon. She is not so
much dressed as richly upholstered. She
is very sure of herself. Yet she is not a
different woman from the* EMILY *we remember; the pity of it is that somehow
this is the same woman.*)

ROBERT (*who makes much of his important
visitor and is also wondering why she has come*).
This is a delightful surprise, Mrs. Ross. Allow
me. (*He removes her fine cloak with proper
solicitude, and* EMILY *walks out of it in the manner
that makes it worth possessing.*) This chair, alas,
is the best I can offer you.

EMILY (*who is still a good-natured woman if
you attempt no nonsense with her*). It will do
quite well.

ROBERT (*gallantly*). Honoured to see you in it.

EMILY (*smartly*). Not you. You were saying
to yourself, ' Now, what brings the woman
here ? '

ROBERT. Honestly, I——

EMILY. And I 'll tell you. You are expecting Mr. Ross, I think ?

ROBERT (*cautiously*).   Well—ah——

EMILY.   Pooh.   The cunning of you lawyers. I know he has an appointment with you, and that is why I 've come.

ROBERT.   He arranged with you to meet him here ?

EMILY (*preening herself*).   I wouldn't say that. I don't know that he will be specially pleased to find me here when he comes.

ROBERT (*guardedly*).   Oh ?

EMILY (*who is now a woman that goes straight to her goal*).   I know what he is coming about. To make a new will.

ROBERT (*admitting it*).   After all, not the first he has made with us, Mrs. Ross.

EMILY (*promptly*).   No, the fourth.

ROBERT (*warming his hands at the thought*). Such a wonderful career.   He goes from success to success.

EMILY (*complacently*).   Yes, we 're big folk.

ROBERT.   You are indeed.

EMILY (*sharply*).   But the last will covered everything.

ROBERT (*on guard again*).   Of course it is a

matter I cannot well discuss even with you. And I know nothing of his intentions.

EMILY. Well, I suspect some of them.

ROBERT. Ah.

EMILY. And that's why I'm here. Just to see that he does nothing foolish.

(*She settles herself more comfortably as* MR. ROSS *is announced. A city magnate walks in. You know he is that before you see that he is* PHILIP ROSS.)

PHILIP (*speaking as he enters*). How do, Devizes, how do. Well, let us get at this thing at once. Time is money, you know, time is money. (*Then he sees his wife.*) Hello, Emily.

EMILY (*unperturbed*). You didn't ask me to come, Philip, but I thought I might as well.

PHILIP. That's all right.

(*His brow had lowered at first sight of her, but now he gives her cleverness a grin of respect.*)

EMILY. It is the first will you have made without taking me into your confidence.

PHILIP. No important changes. I just

thought to save you the—unpleasantness of
the thing.

EMILY. How do you mean ?

PHILIP (*fidgeting*). Well, one can't draw up
a will without feeling for the moment that he
is bringing his end nearer. Is that not so,
Devizes ?

ROBERT (*who will quite possibly die intestate*).
Some do have that feeling.

EMILY. But what nonsense. How can it
have any effect of that kind one way or the
other ?

ROBERT. Quite so.

EMILY (*reprovingly*). Just silly sentiment,
Philip. I would have thought it would be a
pleasure to you, handling such a big sum.

PHILIP (*wincing*). Not handling it, giving it
up.

EMILY. To those you love.

PHILIP (*rather shortly*). I'm not giving it
up yet.   You talk as if I was on my last legs.

EMILY (*imperturbably*). Not at all. It's you
that are doing that.

ROBERT (*to the rescue*). Here is my copy of

the last will. I don't know if you would like
me to read it out ?

PHILIP. It 's hardly necessary.

EMILY. We have our own copy at home and
we know it well.

PHILIP (*sitting back in his chair*). What do
you think I 'm worth to-day, Devizes ?

> (*Every one smiles. It is as if the sun had
> peeped in at the window.*)

ROBERT. I daren't guess.

PHILIP. An easy seventy thou.

EMILY. And that 's not counting the house
and the country cottage. We call it a cottage.
You should see it !

ROBERT. I have heard of it.

EMILY (*more sharply, though the sun still
shines*). Well, go on, Philip. I suppose you
are not thinking of cutting me out of anything.

PHILIP (*heartily*). Of course not. There will
be more to you than ever.

EMILY (*coolly*). There 's more to leave.

PHILIP (*hesitating*). At the same time——

EMILY. Well ? It 's to be mine absolutely,
of course. Not just a life interest.

PHILIP (*doggedly*). That is a change I was thinking of.

EMILY. Just what I have suspected for days. Will you please to say why ?

ROBERT (*whose client after all is the man*). Of course it is quite common.

EMILY. I didn't think my husband was quite common.

ROBERT. I only mean that as there are children——

PHILIP. That's what I mean too.

EMILY. And I can't be trusted to leave my money to my own children ! In what way have I ever failed them before ?

PHILIP (*believing it too*). Never, Emily, never. A more devoted mother— If you have one failing it is that you spoil them.

EMILY. Then what's your reason ?

PHILIP (*less sincerely*). Just to save you worry when I 'm gone.

EMILY. It 's no worry to me to look after my money.

PHILIP (*bridling*). After all, it 's my money.

EMILY. I knew that was what was at the back of your mind.

PHILIP (*reverently*). It's such a great sum.

EMILY. One would think you were afraid I would marry again.

PHILIP (*snapping*). One would think you looked to my dying next week.

EMILY. Tuts.

(PHILIP *is unable to sit still.*)

PHILIP. My money. If you were to invest it badly and lose it! I tell you, Devizes, I couldn't lie quiet in my grave if I thought my money was lost by injudicious investments.

EMILY (*coldly*). You are thinking of yourself, Philip, rather than of the children.

PHILIP. Not at all.

ROBERT (*hastily*). How are the two children?

EMILY. Though I say it myself, there never were better. Harry is at Eton, you know, the most fashionable school in the country.

ROBERT. Doing well, I hope?

PHILIP (*chuckling*). We have the most gratifying letters from him. Last Saturday he was caught smoking cigarettes with a lord. (*With pardonable pride*) They were sick together.

ROBERT. And Miss Gwendolen ? She must be almost grown up now.

(*The parents exchange important glances.*)

EMILY. Should we tell him ?

PHILIP. Under the rose, you know, Devizes.

ROBERT. Am I to congratulate her ?

EMILY. No names, Philip.

PHILIP. No, no names—but she won't be a plain Mrs., no sir.

ROBERT. Well done, Miss Gwendolen. (*With fitting jocularity*) Now I see why you want a new will.

PHILIP. Yes, that's my main reason, Emily.

EMILY. But none of your life interests for me, Philip.

PHILIP (*shying*). We'll talk that over presently.

ROBERT. Will you keep the legacies as they are ?

PHILIP. Well, there's that £500 for the hospitals.

EMILY. Yes, with so many claims on us, is that necessary ?

PHILIP (*becoming stouter*). I 'm going to make it £1000.

EMILY. Philip !

PHILIP. My mind is made up. I want to make a splash with the hospitals.

ROBERT (*hurrying to the next item*). There is £50 a year each to two cousins, ladies.

PHILIP. I suppose we 'll keep that as it is, Emily ?

EMILY. It was just gifts to them of £100 each at first.

PHILIP. I was poor at that time myself.

EMILY. Do you think it 's wise to load them with so much money ? They 'll not know what to do with it.

PHILIP. They 're old.

EMILY. But they 're wiry. £75 a year between them would surely be enough.

PHILIP. It would be if they lived together, but you see they don't. They hate each other like cat and dog.

EMILY. That 's not nice between relatives.

You could leave it to them on condition that
they do live together. That would be a Chris-
tian action.

PHILIP. There's something in that.

ROBERT. Then the chief matter is whether
Mrs. Ross——

EMILY. Oh, I thought that was settled.

PHILIP (*with a sigh*). I'll have to give in to
her, sir.

ROBERT. Very well. I suppose my father
will want to draw up the will. I'm sorry he
had to be in the country to-day.

EMILY (*affable now that she has gained her
point*). I hope he is wearing well?

ROBERT. Wonderfully. He is away playing
golf.

PHILIP (*grinning*). Golf. I have no time for
games. (*Considerately*) But he must get the
drawing up of my will. I couldn't deprive the
old man of that.

ROBERT. He will be proud to do it again.

PHILIP (*well satisfied*). Ah! There's many
a one would like to look over your father's
shoulder when he's drawing up my will. I

wonder what I 'll cut up for in the end. But
I must be going.

EMILY. Can I drop you anywhere? I have
the greys out.

PHILIP. Yes, at the club.

(*Now* MRS. ROSS *walks into her cloak.*)
Good-day, Devizes. I won't have time to look
in again, so tell the old man to come to me.

ROBERT (*deferentially*). Whatever suits you
best. (*Ringing.*) He will be delighted. I
remember his saying to me on the day you made
your first will——

PHILIP (*chuckling*). A poor little affair that.

ROBERT. He said to me you were a couple
whose life looked like being a romance.

PHILIP. And he was right—eh, Emily?—
though he little thought what a romance.

EMILY. No, he little thought what a romance.

(*They make a happy departure, and*
ROBERT *is left reflecting.*)

*The curtain again falls, and rises im-
mediately, as the engraving shows, on the
same office in the reign of King George.*

It is a foggy morning and a fire burns briskly. MR. DEVIZES, SENIOR, *arrives for the day's work just as he came daily for over half a century. But he has no right to be here now. A year or two ago they got him to retire, as he was grown feeble; and there is an understanding that he does not go out of his house alone. He has, as it were, escaped to-day, and his feet have carried him to the old office that is the home of his mind. He was almost portly when we saw him first, but he has become little again and as light as the schoolboy whose deeds are nearer to him than many of the events of later years. He arrives at the office, thinking it is old times, and a clerk surveys him uncomfortably from the door.*

CREED (*not quite knowing what to do*). Mr. Devizes has not come in yet, sir.

MR. DEVIZES (*considering*). Yes, I have. Do you mean Mr. Robert ?

CREED. Yes, sir.

MR. DEVIZES (*querulously*). Always late.

Can't get that boy to settle down. (*Leniently*) Well, well, boys will be boys—eh, Surtees?

CREED (*wishing* MR. ROBERT *would come*). My name is Creed, sir.

MR. DEVIZES (*sharply*). Creed? Don't know you. Where is Surtees?

CREED. There is no one of that name in the office, sir.

MR. DEVIZES (*growing timid*). No? I remember now. Poor Surtees! (*But his mind cannot grapple with troubles.*) Tell him I want him when he comes in.

> (*He is changing, after his old custom, into an office coat.*)

CREED. That is Mr. Dev—Mr. Robert's coat, sir.

MR. DEVIZES. He has no business to hang it there. That is my nail.

CREED. He has hung it there for years, sir.

MR. DEVIZES. Not at all. I must have it. Why does Surtees let him do it? Help me into my office coat, boy.

> (CREED *helps him into the coat he has taken off, and the old man is content.*)

CREED (*seeing him lift up the correspondence*). I don't think Mr. Devizes would like you to open the office letters, sir.

MR. DEVIZES (*pettishly*). What's that ? Go away, boy. Send Surtees.

(*To the relief of* CREED, ROBERT *arrives, and, taking in the situation, signs to the clerk to go. He has a more youthful manner than when last we saw him has* ROBERT, *but his hair is iron grey. He is kindly to his father.*)

ROBERT. You here, father ?

MR. DEVIZES (*after staring at him*). Yes, you are Robert. (*A little frightened.*) You are an old man, Robert.

ROBERT (*without wincing*). Getting on, father. But why did they let you come ? You haven't been here for years.

MR. DEVIZES (*puzzled*). Years ? I think I just came in the old way, Robert, without thinking.

ROBERT. Yes, yes. I 'll get some one to go home with you.

MR. DEVIZES (*rather abject*). Let me stay,

Robert. I like being here. I won't disturb you. I like the smell of the office, Robert.

ROBERT. Of course you may stay. Come over to the fire. (*He settles his father by the fire in the one arm-chair.*) There; you can have a doze by the fire.

MR. DEVIZES. A doze by the fire. That is all I 'm good for now. Once—but my son hangs his coat there now. (*Then he looks up fearfully.*) Robert, tell me something in a whisper: Is Surtees dead?

ROBERT (*who has forgotten the name*). Surtees?

MR. DEVIZES. My clerk, you know.

ROBERT. Oh, why, he has been dead this thirty years, father.

MR. DEVIZES. So long. Seems like yesterday.

ROBERT. It is just far back times that seem clear to you now.

MR. DEVIZES (*meekly*). Is it?

> (ROBERT *opens his letters, and his father falls asleep.* CREED *comes.*)

CREED. Sir Philip Ross.

> (*The great* SIR PHILIP *enters, nearly sixty*

*now, strong of frame still, but a lost man.
He is in mourning, and carries the broken
pieces of his life with an air of braggadocio.
It should be understood that he is not a
' sympathetic' part, and any actor who
plays him as such will be rolling the play
in the gutter.*)

ROBERT (*on his feet at once to greet such a
client*). You, Sir Philip?

PHILIP (*head erect*). Here I am.

ROBERT (*because it will out*). How are you?

PHILIP (*as if challenged*). I'm all right—
great. (*With defiant jocularity*) Called on the
old business.

ROBERT. To make another will?

PHILIP. You've guessed it—the very first
time. (*He sees the figure by the fire.*)

ROBERT. Yes, it's my father. He's dozing.
Shouldn't be here at all. He forgets things.
It's just age.

PHILIP (*grimly*). Forgets things. That must
be fine.

ROBERT (*conventionally*). I should like, Sir
Philip, to offer you my sincere condolences. In

the midst of life we are— How true that is.
I attended the funeral.

PHILIP. I saw you.

ROBERT. A much esteemed lady. I had a
great respect for her.

PHILIP (*almost with relish*). Do you mind,
when we used to come here about the will,
somehow she—we—always took for granted I
should be the first to go ?

ROBERT (*devoutly*). These things are hid
from mortal eyes.

PHILIP (*with conviction*). There's a lot hid.
We needn't have worried so much about the
will if—well, let us get at it. (*Fiercely*) I haven't
given in, you know.

ROBERT. We must bow our heads——

PHILIP. Must we ? Am I bowing mine ?

ROBERT (*uncomfortably*). Such courage in
the great hour—yes—and I am sure Lady
Ross——

PHILIP (*with the ugly humour that has come to
him*). She wasn't that.

ROBERT. The honour came so soon afterwards—I feel she would like to be thought of

as Lady Ross. I shall always remember her
as a fine lady richly dressed who used——

PHILIP (*harshly*). Stop it. That's not how
I think of her. There was a time before that—
she wasn't richly dressed—(*he stamps upon his
memories*). Things went wrong, I don't know
how. It's a beast of a world. I didn't come
here to talk about that. Let us get to work.

ROBERT (*turning with relief from the cemetery*).
Yes, yes, and after all life has its compensations.
You have your son who——

PHILIP (*snapping*). No, I haven't. (*This
startles the lawyer.*) I'm done with him.

ROBERT. If he has been foolish——

PHILIP. Foolish! (*Some dignity comes into
the man.*) Sir, I have come to a pass when
foolish as applied to my own son would seem
to me a very pretty word.

ROBERT. Is it as bad as that?

PHILIP. He's a rotter.

ROBERT. It is very painful to me to hear
you say that.

PHILIP. More painful, think you, than for
me to say it? (*Clenching his fists*) But I've

shipped him off. The law had to wink at it, or I couldn't have done it. Why don't you say I pampered him and it serves me right? It's what they are all saying behind my back. Why don't you ask me about my girl? That's another way to rub it in.

ROBERT. Don't, Sir Philip. I knew about her. My sympathy——

PHILIP. A chauffeur! that is what he was. The man who drove her own car.

ROBERT. I was deeply concerned——

PHILIP. I want nobody's pity. I've done with both of them, and if you think I'm a broken man you're much mistaken. I'll show them. Have you your papers there? Then take down my last will. I have everything in my head. I'll show them.

ROBERT. Would it not be better to wait till a calmer——

PHILIP. Will you do it now, or am I to go across the street?

ROBERT. If I must.

PHILIP. Then down with it. (*He wets his lips.*) I, Philip Ross, of 77 Bath Street, W.,

do hereby revoke all former wills and testa-
ments, and I leave everything of which I die
possessed——

ROBERT.   Yes ?

PHILIP.   Everything of which I die possessed——

ROBERT.   Yes ?

PHILIP.   I leave it—I leave it— (*The game
is up.*) My God, Devizes, I don't know what
to do with it.

ROBERT.   I—I—really—come——

PHILIP (*cynically*).   Can't you make any sug-
gestions ?

ROBERT.   Those cousins are dead, I think ?

PHILIP.   Years ago.

ROBERT (*troubled*).   In the case of such a large
sum——

PHILIP (*letting all his hoarded gold run through
his fingers*).   The money I've won with my
blood. God in heaven. (*Showing his teeth.*)
Would that old man like it to play with ? If
I bring it to you in sacks, will you fling it out of
the window for me ?

ROBERT.   Sir Philip !

PHILIP (*taking a paper from his pocket*)   Here,

take this. It has the names and addresses of the half-dozen men I 've fought with most for gold ; and I 've beaten them. Draw up a will leaving all my money to be divided between them, with my respectful curses, and bring it to my house and I 'll sign it.

ROBERT (*properly shocked*). But really I can't possibly——

PHILIP. Either you or another ; is it to be you ?

ROBERT. Very well.

PHILIP. Then that 's settled. (*He rises with an ugly laugh. He regards* MR. DEVIZES *quizzically.*) So you weren't in at the last will after all, old Sleep by the Fire.

(*To their surprise the old man stirs.*)

MR. DEVIZES. What 's that about a will ?

ROBERT. You are awake, father ?

MR. DEVIZES (*whose eyes have opened on* PHILIP'S *face*). I don't know you, sir.

ROBERT. Yes, yes, father, you remember Mr. Ross. He is Sir Philip now.

MR. DEVIZES (*courteously*). Sir Philip ? I wish you joy, sir, but I don't know you.

M

ROBERT (*encouragingly*). Ross, father.

MR. DEVIZES. I knew a Mr. Ross long ago.

ROBERT. This is the same.

MR. DEVIZES (*annoyed*). No, no. A bright young fellow he was, with such a dear, pretty wife. They came to make a will. (*He chuckles.*) And bless me, they had only twopence halfpenny. I took a fancy to them; such a happy pair.

ROBERT (*apologetically*). The past is clearer to him than the present nowadays. That will do, father.

PHILIP (*brusquely*). Let him go on.

MR. DEVIZES. Poor souls, it all ended unhappily, you know.

PHILIP (*who is not brusque to him*). Yes, I know. Why did things go wrong, sir? I sit and wonder, and I can't find the beginning.

MR. DEVIZES. That's the sad part of it. There was never a beginning. It was always there. He told me all about it.

ROBERT. He is thinking of something else; I don't know what.

PHILIP. Quiet. What was it that was always there?

MR. DEVIZES. It was always in them—a spot no bigger than a pin's head, but waiting to spread and destroy them in the fulness of time.

ROBERT. I don't know what he has got hold of.

PHILIP. He knows. Could they have done anything to prevent it, sir ?

MR. DEVIZES. If they had been on the watch. But they didn't know, so they weren't on the watch. Poor souls.

PHILIP. Poor souls.

MR. DEVIZES. It's called the accursed thing. It gets nearly everybody in the end, if they don't look out.

(*He sinks back into his chair and forgets them.*)

ROBERT. He is just wandering.

PHILIP. The old man knows.

(*He slowly tears up the paper he had given* ROBERT.)

ROBERT (*relieved*). I am glad to see you do that.

PHILIP. A spot no bigger than a pin's head. (*A wish wells up in him, too late perhaps.*) I

wish I could help some young things before
that spot has time to spread and destroy them
as it has destroyed me and mine.

ROBERT (*brightly*). With such a large fortune——

PHILIP (*summing up his life*). It can't be
done with money, sir.

(*He goes away ; God knows where.*)

www.ingramcontent.com/pod-product-compliance
Lightning Source LLC
Chambersburg PA
CBHW011154090426
42740CB00018B/3393